"Today a reader,
tomorrow a leader."
— Margaret Fuller

# This book
# is a gift

**To**

**From**

**Enjoy and Share**

# MICHAEL KOULY

# MUTE

The voices that won't SHUT UP... and you may not know are there!

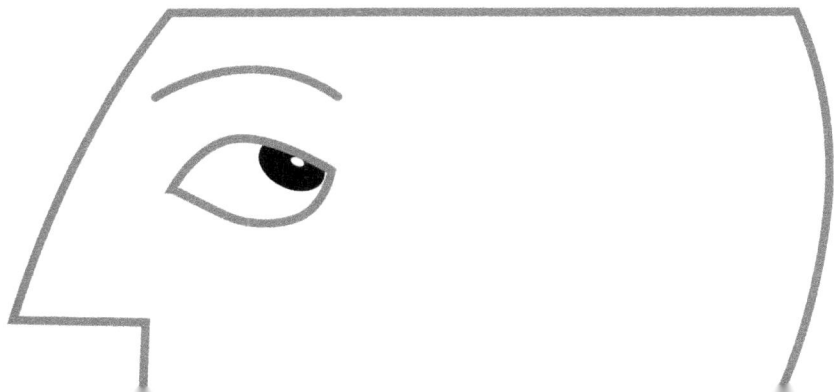

First Edition

**Book 3 of the
Self-leadership Book Series**

ISBN 978-0-9992181-3-6

*To my uncle Dr. Zakaria Kouly for being a remarkable physician, a global thinker, and above all, an inspiring human being.*

# CONTENTS

## *ACKNOWLEDGMENT*

I would like to thank the following good people for their contributions to the creation of this book: Marwa Itani, for translating my thoughts into a clear and elegant sequence of paragraphs and chapters; Mary Shammas, Roy Sayegh, Susan Simons, and Dr. Susan Murray for their feedback on its content and artwork; Mary Shammas for designing the cover, illustrations, and formatting the book for publishing; Roy Sayegh for proof-reading; Devika Brendon and Jo Lavender for editing the book.

I would also like to thank Bill Starnes for encouraging me to write this book for his growing granddaughter Alexandra.

Last, but not least: special thanks goes to all the beautiful voices in my head who keep muting the negative voices and encouraging me to live in line with my purpose.

# *INTRODUCTION*

Would it shock you if I told you that you probably have not made more than one or two decisions in your entire life? What if I told you that many of us will even pass away without making any decisions in our lives that are truly our own? Most of us go through life thinking that each and every decision we have made is ours, and ours alone. BUT! This book is written to shed light on just how many of our decisions are not really our own. The good news? It just requires awareness to start differentiating between our own choices and the choices that are excessively influenced by others.

Dear Reader, when you read the above, you may have started thinking: What is he on about? Is it true? This is crazy!

To answer your concerns, I need to start at the beginning, and introduce 'the voices.' This may sound creepy, but what I am talking about is NOT a set of hallucinations! These are voices that exist within us, within our thoughts and our minds. They are voices of the people in our lives. They are a part of us, yet at the same time have nothing to do with us. Without even realizing it, we are unconsciously being pushed and pulled in various directions by these voices.

We are each made up of a specific genetic code that contains different elements of our personality and a range of core capabilities. Furthermore, we are highly affected by the environment that we are in, and the people that we encounter. The voices address these factors internally and they are present whenever we have an important decision to make. There are many layers of the voices that contribute to what I call our **default self**. This default self affects the way we think, feel, and behave. In other words, it sets our usual way of thinking (e.g. people who by default think everything is a conspiracy), feeling (e.g. some people are always angry or sad), and behaving (e.g. people who always choose to run away from difficult situations).

The default self is reflected in the patterns of our choices, thoughts, interpretations, and behaviors. It is made up of our default perceptions, beliefs (e.g. "family will always be there for me"), values (e.g. "time management is crucial"), worldviews (e.g. "Life is fair"), and patterns of behavior. Furthermore, it is triggered by our current circumstances and the context in which we are operating when we have to make a decision. This default self automatically reacts to situations, and until we are aware of it, and its limitations, it will run our lives. We are often unaware of it, and unconscious of the reasons that cause us to feel and act the way we do.

# THE DEFAULT SELF

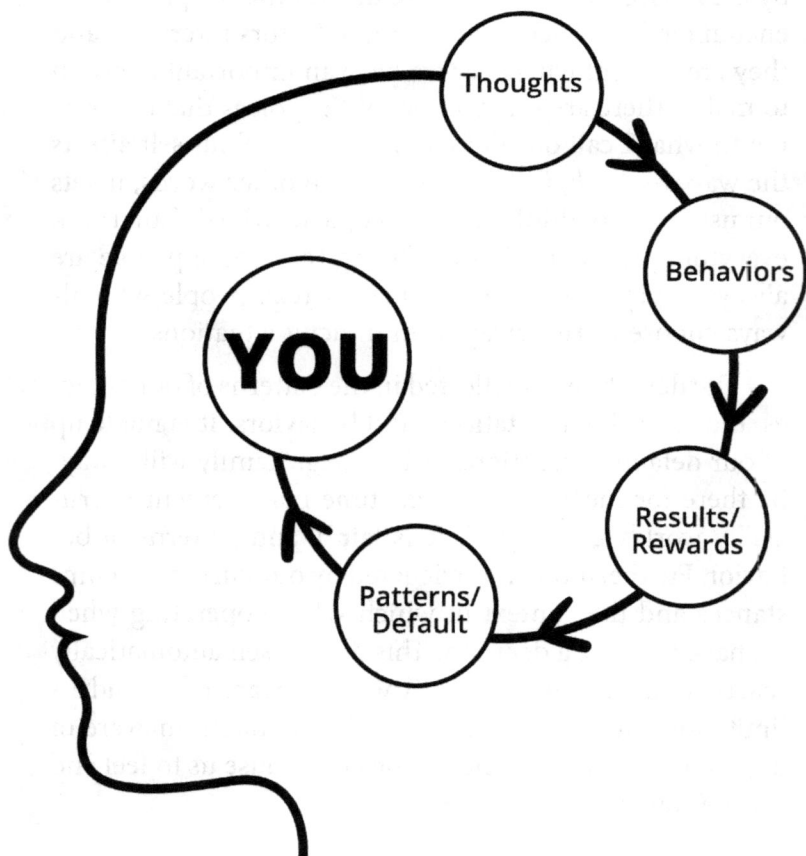

Our voices are made up of two main **influencers:** 1) our DNA, and 2) the people that enter our lives. These two main influencers are then affected by the **experiences** we have had. Eventually, when all three of these components interact enough, they form our **values,** our **worldviews,** and our **hungers**. There is one more layer, and it is probably the most important layer of the voices. This is our voice of **purpose:** this voice is our most authentic version of ourselves. When we start to make our own decisions, we are tuned in to this voice. This is when we actively choose to follow the voice or voices that suit our specific purpose.

The voices play a major role in our everyday lives. Although we are unaware of them, the voices reveal themselves through the small decisions — such as what to eat for lunch — and much larger decisions — such as our choice of career or partner. We can think of their interaction almost like a tug of war. In that conflict, the side that wins is the side that we follow. All of these interactions occur on an unconscious level.

In 2008, John-Dylan Haynes, Chun Siong Soon, Marcel Brass, and Hans-Jochen Heinz conducted a decision-making study. Using brain imaging techniques (functional Magnetic Resonance Imaging), they were able to show that areas in the brain associated with making decisions were activated about ten seconds before the subjects were aware of their decision. This means that they made the decision up to ten seconds before they were aware of it. Since our **decisions happen unconsciously,** it is not until we learn to be aware of these processes, and the various elements that they contain, that we can start to take the crucial steps towards making our own decisions in life.

Keep in mind that although our DNA, experiences, etc., influence and, to a certain degree, make up the person that we are, they should not be allowed to dictate our decisions without our conscious awareness. This is the key difference.

Many of us go through life unaware of the fact that these elements are actually controlling how we react to things. **As soon as we are aware of them and consciously choose to follow one or the other, we can truly say that we have made our own decisions.**

When reading the rest of this book, the question I want you to continuously ask yourself is:

*Which decisions in my life have truly been my own?*

## What Does It All Boil Down To?

Before discussing how we make decisions, it is important to understand two underlying concepts that mark every decision that we make. The first one is *Survival.* Every organism on Earth has an innate need to stay alive. The way that we are structured and created makes us adapt to the environment around us – this is The Theory of Evolution. Survival is key, and the best way to ensure our own survival is to adapt to the different pressures and obstacles that come our way. If we do not fulfill our **basic needs,** they will continuously occupy our thoughts. For example, if we are hungry, we will not be able to focus on other things such as learning or growth. Instead, we will try and find any possible means to quell our hunger.

When we consider Maslow's *Hierarchy of Needs*, the most significant, basic needs have to do with survival. How can we worry about anything else if we are hungry? If we are thirsty? If we are in danger?

Throughout our existence on earth, humans have focused on developing the best ways to survive. Millennia ago, we lived in small groups, hunting for prey, with spears and whatever weapons we could create with our bare hands. From there, we advanced enormously in many different ways. Instead of wooden bows and arrows, we now

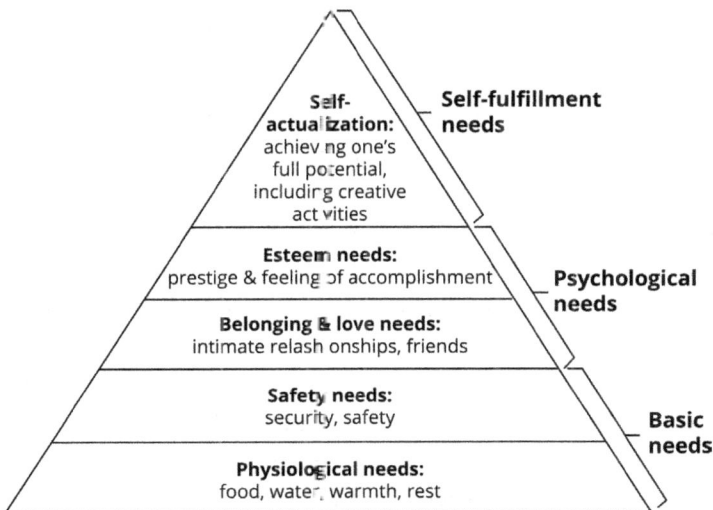

Source: https://www.unicaf.org/maslows-amazing-hierarchy-of-needs/

have guns; instead of riding horses, we now drive cars; instead of hunting for food, we now go to supermarkets or grocery stores. We have found ways to control a world that seemed uncertain and uncontrollable. With advancements in technology, we are no longer victims of our surroundings, but in control of them. In the past, we created systems within chaotic circumstances to ensure that we continuously had abundant supply. These days, for many, getting access to food has become as easy as pressing a button. Our basic survival requirements have been fulfilled, for most of us — but for humans, that is not enough.

In fact, some individuals are going against their survival instinct and are overdosing on drugs or deliberately hurting themselves. Why? Once our survival is guaranteed, humans look for something deeper and more satisfying. It's no longer just about survival: we require the second part of the equation, which is **Growth.**

Growth is tied into a quest for purpose or meaning. Humans have an innate need to strive for something bigger than themselves, to the extent that we would rather not live than live a life that has no meaning. Our brains are more developed than almost all other species on Earth. No other species undergoes philosophical debates. Have you ever seen a giraffe, or any non-human animal, pacing back and forth, contemplating the meaning of life? Non-human animals, once they have ensured their safety, reproductive needs, and food requirements, are generally content. However, when we are hungry, we experience one problem; after we resolve the hunger, we are faced with many more worries and concerns. We strive towards finding meaning and making sense of our lives. We need to feel something is significant, that it gives us motivation to continue and move forward.

According to Victor Frankl, a psychiatrist and the author of *Man's Search for Meaning*, individuals who have something to live for, or who can find meaning in their lives, will survive far longer than others. This point was demonstrated when he discussed his experiences in concentration camps in the 1940s. Those who managed to survive through the traumas were generally individuals who had something to look forward to at home, someone or something to live for. Those who did not have this drive would give up much more quickly.

"There is nothing in the world, I venture to say, that would so effectively help one to survive even the worst of conditions as the knowledge that there is meaning in one's life."

*– Victor Frankl*

Survival and growth go hand in hand. **The more meaning and growth we have in our lives, the more reason we have to survive.** At the same time, if we are worried about our basic survival, we have less time to focus on growth, and it will not be prioritized.

How does this relate to voices? Well, it gives us a background reason for every decision that we make. If we are choosing a job, we focus on something that pays the bills, so that we can survive. If we are deciding on a profession, we need to choose something that will help us survive but also give us meaning, as we may spend most of our lives in this line of work. Therefore, once we have reached a certain level where our survival is not at risk, we will expand our horizons and explore options that provide meaning. If we do not find meaning or passion in what we do, the long hours will feel like years. Survival and growth relate to any decisions that we make, and both influence the voices greatly.

Let us add another layer to this concept. If every human being focuses on survival and growth — imagine a world where everyone consciously contributed to both these aspects — then everything we do will center around these concepts, with our full awareness. Every choice made will be tailored to the survival and growth of everyone. If we focus on co-operation, doing things for the collective good and benefit of others, not at the expense of others' survival and growth, we can elevate everyone around us. We will automatically improve the quality of life for each and every person. This occurs when individuals make their own decisions and are aware of their purpose — their most authentic self — and give their lives meaning.

However, the way we make decisions is far more complicated, with many layers of voices that we will need to consider before we can make decisions which we can truly call our own.

What are the various layers of voices through which we interpret the world around us? Let's explore them in more depth.

*CHAPTER ONE*

# OUR VOICES & US

## Back To The Basics!

> "DNA is like a computer program but far, far more advanced than any software ever created."
>
> *- Bill Gates*

DNA is the voice that we can never get rid of. It has been our longest companion. Before we even drew our first breath, a significant part of who we were going to become was already written in our blueprints, our genes. Think of DNA as the embodiment of all the possible combinations of what we could become. How our lives unfold determine

17

the combinations that will come to pass. Which parts are activated or not depends on the experiences we have, the people we meet, and the decisions that we take. DNA is a beautiful and powerful thing. It is what we are physically made up of, and science in recent years has made major progress when it comes to understanding DNA, but there is still a long way to go.

DNA shapes us, but it is not the sole contributor to our decisions. Think of siblings that have been born in similar environments and have had similar experiences. They can still end up being very different from each other. Conversely, research has shown that identical twins who have been raised apart, and in extremely different environments, still have certain characteristics that are quite similar. Here we see how DNA can shape the way we perceive and interact with the world around us. Does it control everything? Of course not! But to ignore its importance is to be in denial.

Our DNA usually tells our bodies what to do to survive and grow. It is the voice that screams when danger is near. It is the part of us that gets scared if we start to take unnecessary risks. Have you ever seen a video of individuals trying to cross the world's longest glass bridge in China? The bridge is about 1,600 feet long and 715 feet high. From a logical perspective, an individual knows that it is safe, and that in fact highly specialized engineers constructed the bridge to ensure its safety. But as soon as someone steps onto the bridge, logic fails to win out over the fight-or-flight response which kicks in. The whole body responds as if there is danger, tricking us into believing that we might fall. This is just one example of what can happen when the

# THE FIRST VOICE

voice of DNA takes over. It can ring alarm bells and prevent us from taking certain risks that we want to take. At times, its alarms can be false and bring about unnecessary obstacles. At other times, it might save our lives.

The voice of our DNA does not always work on its own. Sometimes certain experiences can trigger fear, and other times an experience might quell it. For instance, if we are afraid of crossing the bridge the first time, and someone drags us across, we are unlikely to feel comfortable crossing it again. However, if we eventually get the courage to cross on our own, the second time we do it, it may be easier. Our feelings often depend on whether our experience was positive or negative. It will either get easier to ignore voice of our DNA (if we had a positive experience), or the voice will get so strong that we will not want to go near the bridge again (if we had a negative experience). This could even extend to fearing other bridges.

Our DNA interacts with our experiences (whether positive or negative) to set the tone for future decisions. How does being aware of this help? Knowing and understanding that the fear that is triggered is just our body's way of protecting us can sometimes help us differentiate between real danger, and a chemical reaction. We will know what the voice of our DNA is telling us, and we can choose whether or not to listen to it.

Besides the survival instinct, research has shown that DNA can also affect other parts of our personality, without us even realizing it. DNA can affect our obedience to authority, and how we deal with stress. These, in turn, will affect the decisions that we make. For example, if we are extremely obedient to authority, we are likely to choose courses which avoid rebellion. We may be less inclined to take risks, so as to not displease authority. If we ask for a promotion and the authority refuses, we will be unlikely to argue about it.

Our DNA also influences how we deal with fear. Some people are born with an increased inclination to be risk-takers by default, while others like to play it safe. For example, let's look at babies. When they are getting ready to take their first steps, some will stand up and start to walk with ease, not really feeling hesitation. Others, when they start to walk, are cautious and careful. At first, they will hold on to couches and tables, just to keep themselves safe and stable. Similarly, the ways in which we deal with fear or the unknown has many effects on the decisions we take. Some people are more keen to take the risky option, to relocate to new countries or to take big leaps without being anxious about such decisions. They are more action oriented, whereas others will feel the need to create a plan, a backup plan, and a backup for the backup plan! Both have advantages and disadvantages: perhaps the risk-taker will get himself into more trouble, while the planner may be too worried to make a move.

Additionally, DNA can affect our temperament. For example, we see babies that seem to smile constantly, and others that appear solemn and serious. These babies may only be a few months old, so the environment has not really made a mark yet — DNA is the main influencer. In another example, there are individuals who we would classify as "hot-headed" (any provocation tends to set them off), while others are naturally calm and not easily provoked. The main factor that affects their temperament is their DNA.

How does this affect our decision-making? If we are naturally moody individuals, some of our decisions may come from impulses. We have to be aware of these moods when making big decisions, so we can stop our temperaments from influencing them too much. For example, if we are angry and feel frustrated with our job, we might decide to quit impulsively. This will have a lasting impact, and should not be a spur-of-the-moment decision. Similarly, impulsive behavior can damage relationships and opportunities, not allowing rationalization a chance to influence decisions.

DNA affects the way we think, feel, act, and function. Have you ever been in situations and thought: 'I am acting exactly like my mother or father?' There is a big possibility that you are because, undoubtedly, you share a few personality traits with them, aside from the role that experience plays. To further this point, when it comes to mental health, one of the first questions that a psychiatrist will ask a patient is whether or not anyone in the family has any form of depression or other disorders. Research has shown that certain individuals are more susceptible to mental illnesses if it runs in the family.

"What are the chances that we will one day discover that DNA has absolutely nothing to do with inheritance? They are effectively zero."

*- Sam Harris*

## *Reflection*

Make a list of:

*   Your Fears
*   Your Traits, negative and positive.
*   Attributes of your Personality
*   Your reaction to Stress, conflict etc.
*   Your temperament

These are some of the aspects that DNA affects. Understanding your natural inclinations will help you gain a better understanding of how DNA will affect your decisions.

The voice of our **DNA** plays an integral part in our decision-making process. This is a voice that we should be aware of, especially in times when we need to go against our natural inclination. Different parts of it are activated from the experiences that we undergo. Our DNA sets our boundaries and the risks that we take. In one way or another, DNA determines a good portion of the road for us. This has sparked a lot of debate throughout the years, and it is sometimes a hard reality to swallow. It is important to note, however, that this does not give us the excuse to use our DNA as a crutch. Remember that DNA is not the only influencer in our decision-making process. There are other significant aspects of our lives that change how we make choices, and it's equally important to be aware of these, including our environments, experiences, friendships, etc.

"We're all going to keep telling love stories, we're all going to tell hero stories. It's all a question of what your own thumbprint, your own DNA, is, and what it brings to the table that makes it unique."

*– Andrew Stanton*

## The People

"Life is similar to a bus ride.

The journey begins when we board the bus.

We meet people along our way of which some are strangers, some friends and some strangers yet to be friends.

There are stops at intervals and people board in.

At times some of these people make their presence felt, leave an impact through their grace and beauty on us fellow passengers while on other occasions they remain indifferent..."

*- Chirag Tulsiani*

Marina Chapman, at five years old, was kidnapped from a village in South America. For unknown reasons, the kidnappers left her in the jungle and the way she survived for five years was by living with a family of Capuchin monkeys. She ate the food that the monkeys dropped, such as berries and bananas; she also demonstrated behaviors that resembled that of the monkeys. She had to adapt to the environment around her and became like the monkeys she lived with.

This is one story among many that demonstrates how the people, or in this case the animals, that surround us can have a major impact on how we see and experience the world. The children in these cases, growing up around animals, end up mimicking the behaviors they see, copying animals such as wolves, wild dogs, or monkeys.

Children are extremely amenable, starting off like untouched clay. They look to their caretakers with wide eyes and copy their behavior because that is all they really know. This demonstrates what an effect the environment or people can have on how we interpret the world around us. If the only beings we see and interact with are animals, then we will behave like them. Part of who we are is considerably dependent on the people who surround us, and teach us what it is to be human.

# FIRST VOICES

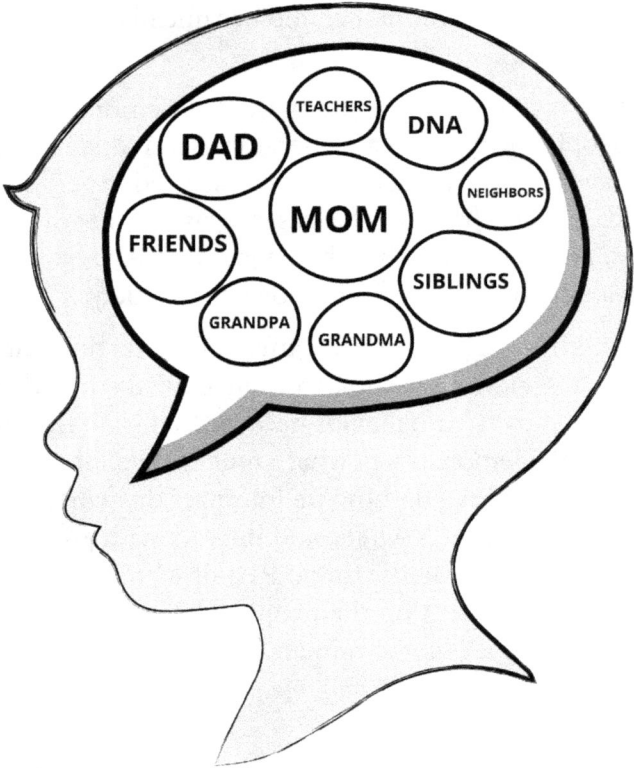

## Bring On The Voices

It is possible to recognize the impact that those around us have, which can sometimes extend so far that we actually end up internalizing their voices. The voices can be seen as programs being installed on a computer, or songs being burned onto a CD. To expand this analogy, think about buying a new laptop or computer. It comes with pre-installed default settings and operating systems. The operating system and all its components are like our DNA. As we install programs and add documents, we affect the way that the computer operates. It is no longer just the factory settings, but the programs added and the way it has been customized that end up changing the way it works. From the start, however, a Mac computer already has different options than a Windows computer, and equally, when we start out our lives, we are all unique, and have a distinctive set of options and opportunities that we can attain with what we are given. DNA plays a large role in determining the shape of our lives, but it does not play the only role, just as a computer's operating system is crucial for it to function , but does not make up its entirety. The programs on the computer (which represent the people around us) dramatically affect its day-to-day running and how it works.

Time after time, the interactions that we have with these individuals give us glimpses of their values and the way they see the world. If they mean a lot to us, some of their beliefs and values can be passed on to us.

Sometimes, we meet an individual just for one week or month, and they teach us a valuable lesson that stays with us forever. In other instances, we will have someone in our lives who is constantly bringing us down, and we are somewhat unaware of how burdensome they have been. It is not until they leave our lives and we feel extremely light that we realize the effect they have had. Whether we want to acknowledge the fact or not, we are impacted greatly by those who surround us. Each one leaves a footprint on our hearts and minds, no matter how long or short their stay.

## *Reflection*

Think about your mind being filled with every single face that you have encountered across your lifetime. Each and every one of us is made up of the faces of those we have encountered.

Make a list of those faces you see. Do not limit yourself to people who are still in your life. Consider other people who you have met, or you know of indirectly (e.g. author of your favorite book). Even be willing to consider fictional characters (e.g. television heroes/heroines, protagonists in books).

It is important that you write all the names of those "faces" down, even if you do not believe that they are one of your voices.

Remember you might not be aware of who influences your decisions.

Now, look over your list and Reflect on:
- Who you feel made (or makes) an impact on your life, whether it is negative or positive.

- With whom do you have a relationship that you value?
- Who do you feel has taught you a valuable lesson which has stayed with you?
- If you were to pick at least five people who played a big role in your life, who would they be?
- Which of the above names do you think might be strong voices?

As we grow, we accumulate voices in our heads. Layer after layer, various voices get introduced. Firstly we will take on the voice of our main caregiver, followed by members of our family, husbands/wives, teachers, mentors, friends, a higher being (God), and colleagues, each according to the culture that we grew up in. Every person that we interact with has the potential to become a voice in our head, and some are louder than others. Their volume depends on what their relationship with us is, and what loyalties we hold towards them. The individuals that are closer to us, and who we feel most loyal to, usually become louder voices in our head. The loudest voice becomes the voice that we least want to disappoint.

"Seek not the favor of the multitude; it is seldom got by honest and lawful means. But seek the testimony of few; and number not voices, but weigh them."

– *Immanuel Kant*

# VOICES MAP

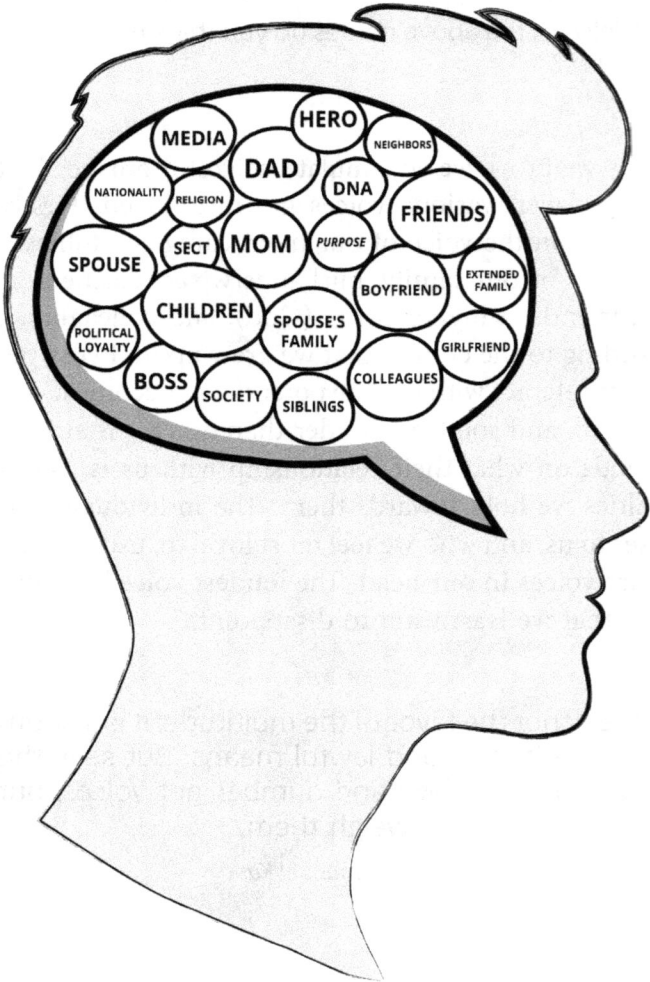

Inside the brain silhouette:
MEDIA · HERO · NEIGHBORS · DAD · DNA · NATIONALITY · RELIGION · FRIENDS · SECT · MOM · PURPOSE · SPOUSE · BOYFRIEND · EXTENDED FAMILY · CHILDREN · SPOUSE'S FAMILY · POLITICAL LOYALTY · GIRLFRIEND · BOSS · SOCIETY · SIBLINGS · COLLEAGUES

## *CHAPTER TWO*

# OUR FIRST EXTERNAL INFLUENCERS

## The First May Not Be the Best... But It Matters!

**The first, most important relationship is the one we share with our caregivers,** for it sets the tone of relationships to come. If we look back to our first interactions, they can explain a lot about the decisions we end up making and the way we see the world.

As we grow up, our first experiences of human interactions and relationships are with our mother, father, or primary caregiver. We are fully dependent on this caregiver to provide us with food, love, and safety. Without this individual in our lives, we are virtually helpless. Interaction after interaction, we as children learn what pleases our caregiver, and what gets us special attention from them. The caregiver's reaction to us also shapes our first experience of judgment and how to deal with others. When the caregiver is not sensitive to our needs, or is consistently not providing attention, we look for other ways to fulfill ourselves. Some of us will start to rebel and act out, while others will learn to detach from the caregiver. On the other hand, when the relationship is a secure one, we will feel safe enough to explore the world around us. Overall, the voice of the caregiver is the first external voice and, therefore, for a long time perhaps, the only really important one. It then gets carried throughout our lives. Let us take the example of Noah.

Noah grew up in a family of four brothers. He was the eldest of his siblings, and his younger brothers were very close to him in age, with a gap of around two years between each. When he was growing up, he always felt that his mother was preoccupied with taking care of everyone else. He felt that he did not get the attention that he wanted. Whenever he wanted something, she would belittle his feelings because she was under constant stress as well, so he carried her voice with him. Whenever he got upset or angry his mother's voice would say: 'Come on, it's not a big deal'; or 'Boys do not cry.' He devalued what he was feeling, and always pushed it aside. When he grew up, and others were vulnerable or emotional around him, he would get very uncomfortable. He was never able to accept his own feelings of sadness and hurt, so it became very difficult for him to accept those feelings in others. His caretaker's voice set the tone for all of his other interactions. It all happened at an unconscious level, and he never realized the extent to which it affected him. He just continued the trend and when he got married and had children, he treated them the same way that he was treated as a child.

These stories are more common than we think. The caretaker's presence in the life of the child, whether they are a mother, father, or other guardian, literally shapes the child and if the effect of their presence is negative, it takes a long time to correct it. The child would need to have many corrective experiences with friends, other family members, and loving relationships throughout their life, in order to see relationships in a different way.

## The Things We Pass On

Let us add another layer: each person that we encounter has a set of their own voices that were passed to them. So, for example, our friend Bernadette has the voices of her mother, father, siblings, cultural obligations, and friends operating in her mind. When she speaks to us or gives us her opinion, she must filter through all of the many voices that affect her. Inheritance is not just about genes anymore. It is also about specific voices, values, and cultural principles— the "programs" that have been adopted into their "default operating systems". In order to understand someone's reactions, or why they behave as they do, we must first decipher the voices that push and pull them. If a person is generally distrustful of all people, this can give us a clear indication of what kind of voices s/he was exposed to, and how harmful the impact on them has been. When we do not understand why an acquaintance or a family member behaves in a certain way, sometimes we can dig a little deeper, and the answer will most likely be in their own voices. In other words, the voices in their minds affect their decisions, as the voices in our minds affect our decisions.

Each person's set of voices also passes on family norms and values. For example, if we grew up in a family that valued cleanliness, this value may be passed on to us. Unconsciously, we will require a clean and neat desk at work, because we will need to operate in an organized environment. This is not necessarily because we were born that way, but because we saw our parent(s) placing great importance on cleanliness. It could be that our mother's voice pops up every time we spill a few crumbs on the floor, or we remember our father used to always ask us to clean our room up if he was going to take us out.

We carry with us the influences that operate on us at different points in our lives. One of the most powerful of these is the influence of a significant other. For example, if your husband or wife constantly compliments the way you look or how you are staying healthy, you may internalize this positive voice. However, as soon as you want to grab a donut, you start to hear their voice change in your head (e.g. 'I thought you were healthy – do you want to damage your health by eating such fatty foods?').

It is important to reiterate that most people do not recognize these voices, as most voices operate on an unconscious level. They do exist, however, and if we do not question them, we become vulnerable to their influence. Like the children who lived with wild animals, we are frequently a reflection of the environment that we are placed in, unless we choose to rise above it.

This is why **purpose** is such an important guiding force, and why it was mentioned at the start. When we understand our most authentic self or the direction that we want to take, we can actively choose the voices that we want to listen to. At the end of the day, the voices that help us adapt, and that are a positive force in our life, are the voices that should remain the strongest. If other voices are hindering our progress and standing in our way, those are the voices that we must let go of. It can very difficult, but once done, it can in fact be one of the most empowering moments of our lives.

## *Reflection*

Looking back at the list of influencers you filled out earlier ("faces" exercise p:28). Take some time to reflect on how they are influencing your life. When you feel you are ready, consider these questions.

Whose voice:

- Do you feel is holding you back?
- Do you feel is pushing you forward?
- Do you think you should hold on to? Why?
- Do you think you should let go of? Why?

## It Is Not All About The Physical!

Craig, when his mother was alive, never really paid attention to what she had to say. He would not take into consideration her opinion about the women he dated, or the way he lived his life. He always tried to live very independently. His mother, unfortunately, developed breast cancer and passed away when he was in his mid-thirties. As soon as that happened, it was as though his whole world turned upside down. Everything that she had tried to get him to do, he started putting into practice. He dated women that she would have approved of. He began watching his cholesterol because she would have wanted him to. Her voice in his head became stronger when she was no longer alive. This could have been due to guilt, but it also served as a way for him to hold on to her just a little longer.

**The voices can live on through other means:** the person does not necessarily have to be alive, and the encounter with that person does not have to be face to face, for it to affect us.

At times, when an individual passes away in the physical world, their voice may intensify or become more strident in our head. For some, this is almost an unconscious way of holding onto the individual. This happens when it is hard to accept that they have passed on. Losing someone close to us is among the hardest things we experience during our lifetimes. It is not easy to recover from loss, especially if the person's voice in our head was already a strong one. It takes time for us to recover, and we never forget, as they will forever be carried with us.

**These are the events in our lives that shake us to the core and rearrange the power of the voices.** These experiences, specifically the loss of loved ones, can make an impactful change in our lives. That is why the experiences that we have can affect how much influence the different voices of the people we encounter, and aspects of our DNA have on our decisions.

A person does not need to be physically present to become a voice in our head. This is how we are able to follow religions, or enjoy stories of past heroes. The extent to which we are affected by others is far reaching. Based on research by Henk Aarts, Peter Gollwitzer, and Ran Hassin, a 2004 article (published in the Journal of Personality and Social Psychology) reveals that people can be motivated and affected by others just by reading about their accomplishments. If we read a story about someone who overcame great odds to achieve their goals, we will be more inclined to attempt this ourselves. We do not necessarily have to witness the success. Just reading about it, experiencing the power of the written word, can affect us. Even music, documentaries, and movies which revolve around human triumphs can affect us on so many levels. The same is true for people who are enormously inspired by saints or prophets. Their physical presence does not have to be encountered; it is their stories that carry weight.

Imagine the impact that important individuals can have on our lives. If we see our parents or close friends succeeding and pursuing their dreams, think about the effect this can have on us. If we see these same people making mistakes and falling apart, the sadness that erupts from them can also take a toll on us. In general, others have the power to either affect us in a positive or negative way, but they do not always have to be present to have an impact.

## You Can't Get Rid Of Me That Easily!

The influence of these significant people does not remain merely on the outside. They actually become part of us, to the extent that if they are not around, we can still hear their voices. For example, I know someone who, to this day, has a severe fear of thunderstorms. Her fear stems from the words of her mother, who believed that a thunderstorm signified Judgment Day had come. When she carried her mother's voice with her, she also carried her mother's fears — she inherited them. Although she could rationalize that nothing bad would happen, on an emotional level, she could not help but feel this fear, because it had been drilled into her mind ever since she was a young girl — it became a part of her mother's voice inside her. The voice of her mother stayed with her, even when her mother had passed away.

The voices that we gather do not go away. They remain our constant companions till the end of time. When the voices become ingrained in our minds, we cannot help but inherit the fears, values, and beliefs of the voices' owners. However, it is time to become aware of them; we cannot deal with something we are not aware of. Once we bring them into the light, everything else becomes a little clearer.

The goal here is not to change the voices, or suppress them, but to become aware of them, so that we can consciously decide which ones to follow… willingly!

> "All higher psychological functions are internalized relationships of the social kind."
>
> *– Lev Vygotsky*

**CHAPTER THREE**

# OUR EXPERIENCES & HOW THEY IMPACT US

## The Experiences

"Character cannot be developed in ease and quiet. Only through experience of trial and suffering can the soul be strengthened, ambition inspired, and success achieved."

*- Helen Keller*

The **experiences** that we have are our ways of challenging the many voices and understanding which ones should be given more importance over others.

Each one of us, from when we were children, has undergone a variety of experiences, and, whether we recognize it or not, each experience has impacted us. From our first steps to the first time we rode a bike, all our successes and failures – all these experiences and our responses to them have shaped the way we see the world around us. Remember the example of the identical twins? Explored in an article in *The Guardian*, two identical twins that grew up in different social classes experienced a different trajectory in their lives. One got better grades in class and was more successful overall, whereas the other left school early. Despite the similarity of their DNA, each one's experiences affected the way their lives unfolded. Therefore, all factors and layers need to be considered, and we need to become aware of their effects on us. Without this awareness, we may go through life being pulled towards things that we are not even interested in doing, but pursue because there are voices within us that push us in certain directions, whether those directions mirror our purpose or not.

**How much weight we place on each of the internalized voices is affected by the experiences that we have**. Did we feel love or abandonment? Were we hit or hugged? All of these various experiences shape how we see the world, and either reinforce some of the voices of other people, or disprove them.

For example, when my son was first starting to swim, I told him to jump in the pool: I reassured him that nothing would happen to him, that he would actually enjoy it. When he jumped in, he swallowed a large amount of water and then looked at me and said, 'see, that is why next time

I won't just jump into the water!' The experience disproved all of the voices that told him to jump, that it would be fun and safe. The next time that he wanted to jump in the pool, it took him a lot longer, and he opted for going down the ladder instead.

Our experiences help clarify the voices better in order to help us make the most out of our survival and growth. For example, imagine significant people in our lives continuously tell us that marriage is the best experience and that it is the only way that we will feel happiness. Without even noticing it, we may adopt this idea until we experience it personally. The true test occurs when we end up getting married. If our experience ends badly and we feel our partner was sent to us from the fiery pits of hell, then we may begin to question the previous advice that we received. On the other hand, if we get married and we feel that it is the perfect match, adding to our happiness significantly, then the voices which suggested that would be the case become stronger.

Each experience can shape and shift the power of the voices, depending on the extent to which the experience affected parts of our life. Imagine, for example, we trust a particular friend blindly and decide to become business partners. As soon as we find out that s/he has been stealing from us, everything changes. This type of experience can have something like a domino effect, making us question all of our relationships and all the people that we have trusted. Why? Because this kind of incident is a heavy betrayal, especially if we never thought it would be possible for this individual to do something like that.

The contrary can occur as well: there are some individuals that we have met and who, for some reason, we are naturally inclined to distrust. It could be that our mother's or father's voice warned us about 'people like that'. However, once we have a positive experience with them, or begin to trust them, the power of the voices shifts. If we grew up, for example, with a racist parent constantly warning us about the dangers of a certain culture, 'those people,' etc., we may by default become racist. It is not until we go out and fall in love with or befriend 'those people' that we realize that our parents had no right to judge them. These kinds of experiences may shock our belief system, because throughout our lives we have been told something, and we have built our entire foundation of beliefs on it. When this changes, it shifts the balance of power. We begin to consistently question the voices that shaped us, such as those of our mother or father. Eventually, this questioning process may open the door to other inconsistencies that may become clear. The impact of a single experience can be very heavy, and tip the scales.

Let's take another example. Perhaps we grew up with a disability, and all of our life people told us what we could and could not do. By default, they underestimated us and did not allow us to do certain things, perhaps out of concern for our health, or lack of trust in our capabilities. If we eventually get fed up with the voices, we will strive to prove them wrong. In order to do so, we will have to work hard and push past our limits daily. There are two possible outcomes. The first is that we are actually able to accomplish more than others expected, and we have the experiences to justify it. This can be very empowering and will break down the walls of negativity. On the other hand, the second outcome may not be so favorable. If we try really hard but are unable to achieve our goals, we may regress even further. Our experiences serve as concrete proof: they are the way that we can actually test the waters and test the voices within. If we shy away from the experiences, we also shy away from proving the voices right or wrong. It is quite an interesting, albeit complicated, dynamic.

## It's Never That Simple!

Nonetheless, some experiences will not do the trick. Some voices are so ingrained within us that even when we experience something contrary to the voice, the voice bites back and remains strong. For example, perhaps we grew up with all the important people in our life continuously criticizing the way we looked and the way we acted. If we grew up being bullied, this negativity would accumulate and eventually cause low self-esteem. Down the line, even if we have corrective experiences, the voices of the bullies (especially if they are family members) might remain strong. Our first voices are crucial, because they are often the strongest and form a base for other voices which come later. It is hard to dismiss a 'first voice' which has been there from the start, when we were a clean slate.

As infants, we are born helpless. We depend on our caregivers, who in in an effort to keep us safe will pass on their voices, values, worldviews etc. Since we are highly impressionable at that age, our early experiences have a stronger impact on us, just as early voices have a stronger impact. For instance, if during our early childhood, we were attacked by the family cat, we might develop a phobia of cats, regardless of our parent's voice reassuring us that the cat means us no harm. In fact, it might be such a strong experience that we carry this fear well into adulthood, unable to shake it off or overcome it without professional help. If this incident was to take place during adulthood instead, we might be less likely to develop a fear of cats, and our parent's voices ('cats mean you no harm') would not be challenged. Later on in life, it becomes harder to have corrective experiences because we have already built the foundation of our current set up. At this stage, we have already created our values and worldviews, and these are more enduring and difficult to change.

Both early voices and early experiences are hard to mitigate. They form the foundations of our beliefs and values, and getting rid of them can be very challenging, at times almost impossible. The old voices will still pop up every now and then, and our experiences will still guide our paths, unless we experience something that is as impactful as the first experience, but completely the opposite.

## *Reflection*

Take some time to consider what you are afraid of. Make a list of those fears. Ready? Now ask yourself these questions:

- Do any of these fears paralyze you?
- Do they inhibit your progress?
- If your answer to any of the two question above is yes, which fears on your list are you thinking of?
- What can you do to let them go?
- What experiences have cemented these fears?
- Whose voice(s) stops you from facing your fears? (think of the people in your life)
- Whose voice(s) encourages you to move past your fear?

In a more sensitive yet impactful example, if a girl is abused by her father as a child, she will start to distrust men in general. When she grows up, if she finds a man that is actually able to make her feel safe and sees the beauty within her, connecting with this person could be a healing experience for her. It would take a long time to build that trust with this individual, but if she is able to and builds new experiences with him, this may allow her to slowly disconnect from her previous beliefs and experience. It would take a long time to push past the years of distrust and to slowly let this person in. However, she might be able to, as long as there is consistency and they have built enough experiences together to counteract the first experience. Then she will be able to move past it.

The voice is sometimes a strong positive one that counteracts negative experiences. For example, Meryl Streep went to a variety of auditions where she was rejected, and at one point was told that she was not pretty enough. Had her experience dictated what she would do, she would never have tried again, but she had a strong voice of perseverance that served her well in this situation. After a difficult time breaking into film, Meryl Streep went on to receive a record-breaking 21 Academy Awards.

Some voices within us tell us to keep pushing even if we fail. There are many success stories that show how important it is for people to fail in order to rise above that failure. Had their experiences dictated their decision, they would have never moved forward. Princeton Professor Johannes Haushofer, in an article in *The Guardian,* describes how he courageously posted a resume filled with all of the positions that he applied for and did not get. In other words, it was his "resume of failures." He wrote this document, he claims, to "give some perspective", as most people just see the successes that others achieve, not the hard road of failures and disappointments that they must face in order to get to where they now are. His "resume of failures" may affect many others and could be the voice that they need to hear to move past their difficulties, to give it one more shot.

When we realize that other people have passed through hard times just like us, it becomes easier to move past these difficulties. The experiences that we go through are still hard to navigate, but when a voice is strong enough, it can propel us past any experience. This contrasting positive voice might be the voice of a caretaker or a friend who has continuously supported us and believed in us. It could also be the pull of purpose. Once clarified, our purpose can push away even the worst of experiences.

## *Reflection*

Take a moment to reflect on incidents in your life where other peoples' ability to overcome their failures has helped you do the same. Think of people you know personally, people you have heard about, or famous individuals that you find inspiring.

Reflect on:

- Were there times when you felt like things could not get better, but something within you kept you going?
- Can you remember whose voice is responsible for this?

It is paramount to realize the subtle impact that each experience has on us. Sometimes it takes a lot to offset a strong voice. It really depends on the how powerful the impact of either the experience or the voice is. This all boils down to how much emphasis we ourselves place on a particular voice or experience — what we perceive to be important.

### *Reflection*

Up to this point, are there any thoughts or perceptions that you have changed as a result of reflection, introspection, or new experiences?

- What voices did you challenge or change?

- What voices do you think you will need to challenge now?

# The Experiences That Change Us All

There are certain experiences which could shake any of us to our core, no matter how strong the voices or other parts of us are. These are the kinds of experiences that trigger elements of helplessness and shame, or, on the other end of the spectrum, the types of opportunities that place us in a position where we are given a huge amount of responsibility and/or freedom. These experiences will test us to the extreme and push us to our limits. After these experiences, we will change – either for the better or the worse.

### *Reflection*

Think about your life up to the point you read this sentence.

- What experiences have you had, good or bad, that proved to be a turning point in your life?

- Did you experience any wake-up calls or "Aha" moments, where an experience helped you make sense of the world around you? Describe them.

For most of us, becoming 18 is a turning point in life. It is the time when school is over and the path that was drawn out for us until then ends. Previously, most decisions would be made for us; at school we would not always get to choose the subjects we studied or the projects we took part in. Once we reach 18, however, and face the daunting reality that we are almost a full-time adult, choices suddenly appear. We have so many options which have opened up: Go to college? Take a year off? Start work? If we decide to go to college, there are endless types of universities that we can choose from, not to mention the myriad of majors that are out there. There are universities at home, abroad, or even online. This is one of those decisions that many people will start to panic about. The entire family dynamic changes. Perhaps we will move away, or assert more of our independence. We will end up meeting so many more people, and therefore have more potential voices to internalize. If we start college or work, we will be surrounded by an entirely new set of people, and even more so if we move into shared accommodation. This shift in responsibility can shake all the rest of our experiences. It is the first time that we do not have our caretaker to lean on.

In some bird species, when a baby bird hatches from its egg, the mother bird does not wait long to throw it off the cliff! It is in that crucial moment that it is either 'bird enough' - or not! Will it fly? Or will it fall? These are crucial moments when a major decision must be made, the moments where we can either make the most of the opportunity we are given, or close ourselves off. In any major decision, there is a **tug of war** between the voices. It is in these experiences, the big ones, that the power of the voices shifts, and leadership is up for grabs.

It is at these crucial moments that you will experience a turning point in your life. It is possible that a minor, or completely new, voice will become dominant. When we are moving out of the house and asserting our independence, perhaps our caretaker's voice will no longer be the loudest. Maybe it will be the voice of our roommate, or perhaps other people we meet along the way. It is definitely in times of change that we take a pause and rearrange the balance of the voices. Perhaps for some, it will remain the same, but for others these experiences might lead to a rearrangement of the voices.

The experiences that really alter the balance are those that test our sense of control in the world. The above example was an experience that related to a certain period of time when we needed to make our own decisions and assert our opinions. Normally, this will happen at a time when we have been given a lot more control. If we are moving to a new environment and are surrounded by new people, that can also make us feel less in control until we adapt to our surroundings. Of course, there are other events that can be disorienting because they literally hijack our sense of control. For instance, some experiences can shatter our sense of safety and bring about feelings of helplessness — sexual assault, torture, or being in a conflict situation and witnessing a lot of violence and death. It is in these moments, when all forms of control are lost, that we start to doubt everything, and our clear understanding of safety no longer exists. Our own body becomes foreign to us, perhaps surreal, and no longer belongs to us.

## Why Is Control So Important?

At the end of the day, a core element of survival is having the ability to control our surroundings. Therefore, when we encounter experiences that make us doubt our sense of control, or place us in a state of confusion, major shifts can happen.

Most of the time, we are blissfully unaware of some of our internal voices. Nevertheless, there are times when tension and stress are caused specifically because we are confused about a decision. Usually, this happens when we are in situations where:

1- The power of the voices on each side is equal, and we are really not sure which to choose, and in what direction it will take us. For example, imagine we call a family meeting, and each of our family members is a voice. On opposite sides we have an equal number of important members voicing their concerns. Let us assume that the topic of the meeting is getting married. Some of the people in our lives are strongly in favor, while other are equally against it. How can we resolve the standstill?

One way this happens is if the circumstances change. For instance, one of the important voices is no longer there (e.g. a key family member passes away). Now the scales have shifted, and one side will be dominant, and we will follow that voice(s). Another way this could be resolved is if one of the dominant voices switches sides. For instance, if during our family meeting, a parent decides to no longer oppose the marriage, this will shift the voices towards the supporting side — which is now dominant — and we will go ahead with that decision. Another option is if we introduce our own unique, authentic voice into the mix, the one that shifts the balance towards the decision that best suits us, and not the other voices. In this situation we hear, or know, what each voice is going to say. Then we consider what decision best suits our lives. It will mute all the other opposing voices, we can resolve the standstill, and make the choice that is in line with our own authentic self.

2- What we once thought was certainty becomes unsure, meaning that a 'coup' in our head is imminent, and we are not quite sure who will take the lead now. We are patiently waiting for the elections to take place! This happens during moments of sudden change and/or shifts in control (remember the example of moving out), or when we experience challenging moments, ones that we hope never to encounter (e.g. terminal illness). It is when experiences shake us to the core that there is often a major shift among the voices. At this point, the foundations on which we are basing our lifestyles, beliefs, worldviews, or values have been shaken.

To begin to resolve this confusion, we will need to reassess how we make sense of our lives. We will have to find a new way of living which allows us to move on and grow. Let us consider the example of Ric Elias, a survivor of the plane crash in 2009. In his TED conference talk, he discusses how almost dying forced him to reassess his life. He realized how much time he had wasted engaging in petty conflicts, letting his ego and need to be right get in the way of his happiness, and putting off experiences he wanted to have. This major event shook the foundations of his lifestyle and caused him to reconsider what mattered most to him. His authentic voice took the lead.

In another example, imagine a person who does everything "right", but one day s/he is diagnosed with lung cancer. S/he does not smoke and lives a healthy lifestyle. This will shake their worldview that "if you do live healthy, you will live a long life". Suddenly, s/he cannot make sense of what has happened and ends up reconsidering their worldview. It is when s/he is able to find a suitable interpretation for what has happened that they will be able to move forward with their life and decide whether or not to try and fight the disease. The point is that we may encounter situations where the very foundations of our lives are stripped away from us, and then we will begin to question which voice to listen to. It is when we find a new satisfactory interpretation, whether it is a belief, worldview, value, etc., that a voice will become dominant over the others. This way we resolve this confusion, adapt, and move on with our lives.

**3-** There is a new element that potentially shifts the balance of the voices. There will be times when the voices in our heads will be pushing and pulling, and we will not know which one to listen to. Confusion ensues, and we do not know which decision to make. Then a new element is added to the mix, a new source of information that shifts the voices and further complicates the decision. Let us revisit the family meeting example. Imagine that as the voices are debating for and against the marriage, we discover that our partner is pregnant. Now, we suddenly have to think about a child, which was not part of the previous equation. In this case, the new information may either shift the voices one way —resolving the issue — or it may introduce a new voice into the mix that becomes dominant and resolves the issue.

The point is that there will be some situations, in every human life, where everyone would go through some transforming experiences. Whether they produce positive or negative changes, these certain experiences will get to our cores and shift the power of our voices.

For example, let us assume that we fall in love with people who have values or worldviews that oppose some of the ones we have acquired in our lives. The love we feel for these individuals will make them a strong voice in our minds. It is possible that when one of these individuals asks us to do something that goes against the dominant voices in our minds, a tug of war will begin. We will be confused about what to do. If we choose to side with the voice of the person we love, we risk upsetting our other significant voices — which may include our other loved ones (e.g. family). If we side with our earlier voices, we may risk losing the person we love. The experiences we go through with these individuals have shifted the scale, and their strong voice will make us question some of our earlier voices. It is possible that their voice may become the dominant one, shifting the scales to their side, and we will start to make decisions based on it.

# VOICES AT WAR

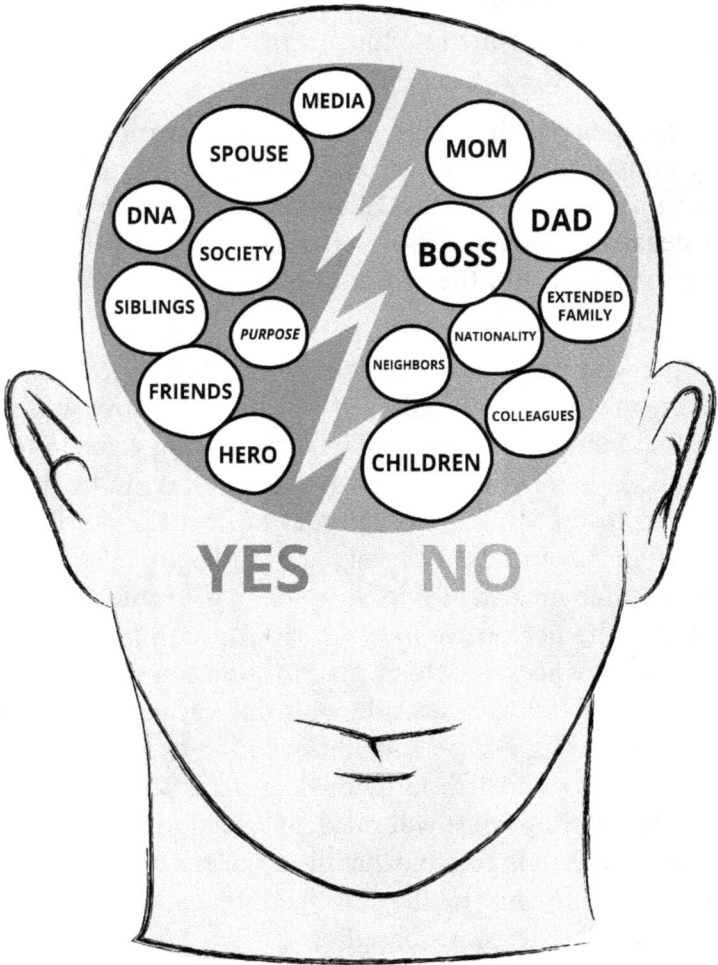

## *Reflection*

Consider the major moments in your life, whether they are good or bad. List them. Now, think about if and how these experiences may have shifted your perspective (for instance, did you ever find yourself saying, "my mother was right after all!" or something along those lines?).

- Did you find that something changed?
    - o How did it change?
- Now, considering the people in your life:
    - o Did your relationship with some grow stronger? Weaker?
    - o Did you remove some people from your life?
    - o Did you introduce new people into your life?

# A Change Is A-Coming!

There is a constant dynamic that needs to be mentioned. The balance between our voices is always shifting and changing. Usually, it happens without our awareness. As we grow older, the changes or shifts become less and less significant, but they still occur. Our voices become more ingrained, especially if experiences confirm them, and it can take something quite extreme to shake them. When we are young, the voices have not been interacting for as long, but as time goes on, the interactions create various filters, and we start to see the world through these colored filters.

When we are aware of the voices, we can choose to feed the ones that provide us with stability and safety, and we can choose to starve those that plant fear in us without a proper cause. We can choose to listen to the voices of encouragement and ignore the voices of criticism, but we need to be aware that they exist, and we need to be aware of the effect that they have on us. That makes all the difference to our happiness!

*CHAPTER FOUR*

# OUR RESPONSES SHAPE OUR LIVES

## The Created Filters

The next parts that will be discussed are not necessarily separate internal voices but are created due to the interactions between our DNA, the voices of people that we encounter, and the experiences that we have. They are the following: our *values*, our *worldviews*, and our *hungers.*

We start to develop our values from the people that have the biggest impact on us. When our experiences continuously show us that these values help us survive and grow, they become cemented and a part of our own value system. These values in turn become the filters that we use to judge the varying voices, and how much importance we would like to place on each of them. If a voice goes against our values then it will not have much importance in interactions to come, unless we have an experience impactful enough to shift the value. Similarly, we adopt worldviews from the significant people in our lives as well as from our experiences and interactions with our surroundings. Worldviews are our perspectives on the world and our beliefs about how the world works. They are the stories we tell ourselves that color how we see the world. This will affect how we interact with and interpret the world around us and make decisions.

Lastly, our hungers are created when there is a lack of interaction between our experiences and the people we have in our lives. As stated earlier, each decision boils down to two aspects: survival and growth. Our hungers arise when we do not achieve certain milestones in our survival or our growth. When we grow up in a household that lacks love, this starts to form an emptiness inside us, which expands. This may get to a point where our hunger for love shape our experiences as what we compulsively seek to attain leads our decisions. So, let's take a look at the various filters…

## Filter One: Our Values

When she was a little girl, Amber was told that if she was going to succeed in life, she needed to be the best at everything. If she got a 90 on an exam, her parents asked her why she did not get a 95. If she cooked something, they would complain that there was not enough salt. If she picked a three-leaf clover and gave it to them, they would look at it with disdain and say, "Why not four?"

In rare moments, they would praise her greatly for being at the top of her class, or doing something exactly right. Amber thus learned that, for her to survive, she must attain perfection. She went through school as an honor student and passed college with flying colors. But then it happened… Her first failure.

Amber was not so good at perfecting things in a work-place filled with what she saw as 'imperfect' people. She grew frustrated and angry. When she had to work on team projects, she would spend extra time just fixing everyone else's work because she could not let it go. Her work started to falter as the deadlines piled up and she could not meet them because she was perfecting work which was really Bob's from accounting, or Molly's from marketing.

Eventually, her boss could not handle it anymore. Amber was forcing everyone to work overtime due to her obsession with minuscule details, and she was not focusing any longer on the bigger picture. He had to make a decision and Amber was fired. She had never imagined that she could receive an F at her job, but she did. When that happened, it was like her neatly pressed life got all wrinkled up. She felt like she herself was a failure. After she got fired, Amber spent weeks going back to the office, begging for her job back. She told them she would work faster, harder, and better. She got so persistent about getting her job back that her previous boss had to file a restraining order against her.

Perhaps this story is a bit extreme, but the point is to take a look at what really happened. Amber, as a child, was always told by her parents that she was not good enough, that the only way she was "worthy" was when she succeeded and did well. Amber's experiences with her parents led her to value perfection. It became so ingrained that anytime something was less than perfect, the voices of her parents would filter through this value and make her feel like she had failed.

Amber, growing up, internalized that voice and worked harder than most. In school and university, she was able to keep up the façade of perfection, as she worked night and day. This kept her weak self-image afloat because she was succeeding, her parents were proud, and to her that meant she was worthy of respect and admiration. When it came to her job, however, she could not let small mistakes go because any mistake poked at her already sensitive value. Eventually, as with most humans, the idea of being "perfect" came crashing down. She was left with a big F, the voices of her parents were screaming, and she felt worthless.

Let's take a deeper look at values. From our experiences, our DNA, and the people that we encounter in our lives, we slowly start to build up our value system. Our values can be defined as the objects, relationships, people, and principles that we hold in high regard, and that we place great emphasis on. They are the things and people that we dedicate most of our time and resources to. Furthermore, they can become our moral compass, giving us direction on what we believe is right and what we believe is wrong.

Most children will adopt the value systems that their parents hold, because, for them, their parents are the most influential beings in their life. Our values, similar to our cultures and religious beliefs, get passed on to us by others that have impacted our life greatly.

## *Reflection*

Take some time to reflect on your key values. What concepts do you value most in your life? Write them down.

Lawrence Kohlberg, an American psychologist, proposed a theory of moral development. At the start of life, until about 9 years old, a child's moral compass is defined based on what they are punished for, and also a sense of what benefits them as a whole. As the child starts to reach adolescence and verges on adulthood, it becomes a matter of rules and social norms. Once we become adults, only about 10-15% of individuals, according to Kohlberg, go beyond the rules and base their sense of morality on their own conscience and universal principles, rather than on social norms. This percentage indicates that morality can exist beyond the rules.

The theory of moral development stipulates that we are highly affected by the people that are introduced into our lives, and the systems that we belong to. The caregivers we have and the society we are part of become our models, and thus our values are highly influenced by those in our inner circle, and societal pressures.

Aside from the influence of others, our own experiences are added into the mix. This can be seen when we as children realize that 'Mommy and Daddy aren't always right.' For example, if we were overly protected in our home environment, we may have adopted a fear of taking risks — we might value "control" and "discipline". When we finally have to take our first steps outside this environment and actually need to take risks, we may realize that other environments are not so controlled and disciplined and this may trigger a chain reaction, making us question what other values are not "true". Nonetheless, it will take a few experiences to prove the strong voices wrong and create a new value. Our experiences constantly shape how we interpret our environments, and in turn shape our values. When the voices and experiences that we encounter become strong enough, they become part of our value system, and sometimes an experience may force us to change our values.

For example, it might be that we grew up believing that lying is a sin and that we should never lie. But then one day, we make a large mistake on a huge project at work, and we know telling the truth would mean losing our entire livelihood, while lying will solve the problem without doing any harm. If we have extra responsibilities like children, there is further pressure to keep the job, and so we end up lying. What happens when a person who has been taught never to lie tells a lie? It causes a lot of dissonance. We start to feel guilty, and the fight between our internal conflicting voices ensues. Thoughts like: "I am a bad person," "I am a liar" will start to flood our minds. These harsh criticisms may continue until we are able to either forgive ourselves for this single transgression, or decide that we value "family" and "security" more than we value "absolute honesty". In other words, we either accept that this is one incident and we work to make sure we do not transgress this value, or we shift the importance of this value within us. If we are unable to shift the importance of what we value, the dissonance will continue and we will not feel a sense of stability. It may become quite difficult to live a life where the voices within are constantly pulling and pushing us in so many different directions.

The way we were raised reflects to a certain degree the values of our caregivers, and plays a major role in shaping our own **values.** If we were raised in an extremely permissive household, we may grow up not valuing rules or understanding the importance of these rules. Let's consider George. George as a child was never given proper boundaries. His room was filled with hundreds of toys, because whenever he requested something, his parents couldn't bear to deprive him of it. He would not play well with other children because he never learned the concept of sharing, and believed that whatever he wanted he would get. He did not have a set bedtime and would be up playing with his toys until he got sleepy. When he became a teenager, he never really was disciplined enough to study hard or do well in school; he would study when he felt like it. This lack of understanding of boundaries was carried with him to adulthood. As an adult, he could not keep a steady job; he would get angry when people did not behave in the exact way he wanted, and it was difficult for him to maintain relationships.

This, once again, is a more extreme example, but it is meant to draw out the point clearly. If, conversely, a child grows up in a household where the type of parenting is authoritarian, the child may grow to value the word of authority and even develop an element of fear towards authority and the rules. They may believe what makes them 'good' or 'bad' is how well they follow these rules. For instance, Lily grew up in a household where, if her father asked her to jump, she would ask how high. There was no room for misbehavior, as severe punishments would follow. It was a household that focused more on rules, rather than showing love. Lily was never really in tune with what she felt because it often was disregarded. How she was treated was more about what she did than how she felt. Her parents set so many rules and regulations that she felt most of the time she was living in a military base. As she grew up, she never really trusted her own judgments, and was always worried about what authority figures thought of her. She was very careful about what she said and did not say. She was also an overachiever, because she was taught to follow rules rigorously. She valued rules and regulations, and she passed on the same lessons to her children.

Therefore, the surroundings that we grow up in and the values that our parents model for us truly create and affect the basis of the values that we adopt. That is why research shows that an environment that provides elements of love and nurture as well as structure and consistency is the optimal environment in which a child can grow and build a healthy and secure attachment to others, and a strong sense of self.

It is not only the caregivers, however, that can influence our value system. Many other factors can act like internal voices. These might be our culture, or our religious beliefs. We have all grown up in certain cultures, and many of us will have followed religious practices in our households. Our cultural traditions and religious practices give us a sense of control in a chaotic world. They give us ways of making sense of the world around us, and provide feelings of security and stability. In terms of voices, cultural and religious traditions give us certain regulations to live by, and set standards that we must abide by. This satisfies our need to belong, and helps us feel like we are part of something bigger than ourselves. Needing to belong stems from an underlying survival need, and allows us to live with one another in stability, peace, and harmony.

We can project the voices on to a larger framework to understand this a little better. Think of the entire world as one entity — Earth — and see each individual as being an internal voice of Earth. The religions that we practice are like the value systems that we have, and the culture is like the worldview. Certain religions and cultural practices die out when they stop being of benefit to us, and when they no longer contribute to our survival and growth, but significant changes can take thousands of years to occur when we consider that each of Earth's internal voices must change

If we look at each individual separately, we can see that it takes a long time to change the value system, but that it does happen when the belief system no longer provides the benefit that the individual is seeking. Let's consider the changing perception of women in society. For a long time, it was beneficial to label women as caretakers, their main role being the protectors of their children. However, there has been a shift in this role. There are a lot of working mothers, women are striving for equal pay and rights, and cultural evolution is slowly happening. The image of women is gradually shifting, and it changes other images as it does so – for example, we now have stay-at-home fathers as well. We are valuing "equality" more than we did in the past, so much so that the roles and expectations of the genders are starting to evolve and change. It is taking a long time, but with enough experiences and examples of it working out, the shift will continue to progress.

## Two Types of Values

There are two types of values that we can adopt: we have the current values that we possess, and the values to which we aspire. The current values are the ones that make up our default setting: they determine how we react to certain things, and what we place value on in the present moment. Perhaps one of the main values many of us share is career success and work drive. Our aspirations are the values that we are working towards, the values that we wish to have. Perhaps, if we are currently single, one of our aspired values is "family". While we want a family life, it is something to achieve later on, something to work towards slowly.

At times, the two types of values can create internal conflict: if we see ourselves acting against the values we aspire to for the sake of values we currently hold, it can trigger alarmed voices. Perhaps we are so work-driven that we do not have enough time to meet new people. What if we reach a certain age, and the possibility of a family becomes less and less feasible? These are all things that can create conflict between the voices. It is important to recognize both our current values, and the ones that we aspire towards, because both influence the voices.

For example, the voice of our mother might say: 'Time is passing, and you are no closer to getting that family.' Equally, the voice of our boss might say: 'You can become head of the division; you just have to give it all you have got.' Both of these voices are important because one represents a current value, which is achievement and success at work, whereas the other represents an aspiration. Consider the following: if we are continuously late to everything, we have a problem organizing our time. If one of our aspired values is "time management", every time that we run late, we will trigger alarm bells and start to feel uneasy. The voice of our mother might come up: 'You are always late', while the voice of our partner or friend could say: 'Looking good means feeling good, and it is important to take the extra time.' We end up being late because we value one voice over the other, but, nonetheless, it will still cause worry and annoyance as we aspire to manage our time better and feel organized.

Therefore, it is essential for each of us to reflect upon what is **really important to us**. It is about delving deeper into the various layers of who we are to discover more and more. If we understand more about our own values, our perspectives when making decisions will become much clearer.

## *Reflection*

Create a list of your top 10 priorities and rank them, starting with the most important one.

Now take some time to consider:

• Why did you rank them in this order?

• Are they in line with the key values you listed earlier?

Let us take this a step further. I want you to consider if these are in line with your current values? Or with your aspired values?

Considering only your aspired values, would you:

• Change the ranking order of your priorities?

• Would you remove any priorities?

• Would you introduce new priorities?

A final point: when the old values or interactions do not work, shifts become a necessity and are bound to happen. But values are sometimes stubborn, and will need more than just one voice or one experience to undergo change. The values are based on an accumulation of important voices and experiences, so imagine trying to remove that filter. It can be a real challenge, but it is not impossible!

# Filter Two: Our Worldviews

Have you ever noticed that some people in your life, no matter what you tell them, can turn it into something negative? There are others who, no matter what tragedy befalls them, can turn their experiences into rainbows and sunflowers? These perspectives are largely related to the worldview that each and every one of us adopts.

Our worldviews, in the simplest of terms, are how we see the world. After we have been influenced by people and experiences, we develop specific filters through which we interpret the world around us; these give us each our unique perspectives. Because of these perspectives, we make certain decisions and act in certain ways. For instance, what if I were to ask you what first comes to mind when you think of men or women? Some people would say: "Men are dogs" or "Men are liars", while others would say: "Men are strong", or "Men are kind." The same can be applied to women. Some may say: "Women are gold diggers" or "Women are catty"; on the other hand, some would say: "Women are elegant" or "Women are intelligent."

If most of the things that come to our minds are negative, that says a lot about how we see the world. This is equally true if many of the words that we come up with are positive.

How do our worldviews develop? Mostly from the things that we experience and the influencers in our lives, and how we learn from them. For example, the individual that associates the word 'women' with something like 'gold diggers' may have had most of their experiences shaped by something negative with women. Perhaps that person had a horrible experience with a woman that dated him/her for money. The experience might have been extremely devastating, and from there the individual has started to generalize their feelings and apply them to all women, believing that none of them can be trusted. This experience — because it was very profound and affected the individual greatly — shaped part of their worldview.

It could also be one of the voices that they internalized. Let's say that this individual grew up with a mother that was never there, and a father who used to tell him stories about how his wife, the child's mother, cheated on him and left him with no money. The child will internalize the voice of his father, and may view women with distrust and disdain, as he never grew up with a more positive example. From this one story, he will generalize his viewpoint of all women, in order to protect himself. Perhaps subconsciously, he wants to avoid the same thing happening to him.

Similarly, individuals who see life as difficult and unyielding may have this worldview due to a variety of experiences. If a person underwent some form of physical or sexual abuse by family members, it can be very difficult for them to move past this abuse and find security and happiness. They may have shaped the rest of their experiences through the lens of this abuse, and this may taint any future experiences. Alternatively, this individual might have grown up in a very poor household. They would have seen other children playing with high tech games and being given opportunities that they could never have dreamed of.

Right from childhood, they may have adopted the viewpoint that "Life is unfair, other children get things that I do not have", or "I have to work twice as hard in order to get something which other children are just given." Similarly, if these children have grown up with a single parent, or in the foster system, they may look at what other children have and adopt the viewpoint that they are at a disadvantage.

These experiences and internalizations slowly form into worldviews. Eventually, the child that compared themselves to others and felt that the world was unfair might adopt a helpless attitude. They might feel that there is no point trying to work hard because they would never be able to catch up or bridge the gap between themselves and others who went to a premium high school and could afford a top-tier college.

Let us look at another example. Consider someone who has grown up on the coast, where there was a seemingly endless amount of fish, and the fertile soil provided plenty of fruit and vegetables. This person's experiences may lead them to form a worldview of abundance, the idea that there "will always be food when you need it", and that "the world provides us with more than we could need". It may become so ingrained that they believe that whatever they need will be available and provided to them.

In other instances, our religious beliefs can be a strong source of worldviews. We may believe that "life is fair" or that "if you do good, you will be rewarded in kind". A few of our core beliefs about how the world functions come from our religious and cultural beliefs. If our experiences tend to support these worldviews, they will become more firmly fixed in our minds, and will affect how we see the world and make decisions.

Our worldviews affect the way that we see opportunities, and shape our attitudes when it comes to pursuing them. If we return to the "life's not fair" individual who didn't see a point in pursuing their goals because they were at a disadvantage, we can see how an alternative worldview might have led to a very different outcome. If they grew up believing that hard work would always pay off, they might resort to extremes in getting a diploma and achieving a place into a top-tier school. They might overcome all the obstacles in their path because they did not define who they were based on their circumstances.

The difference between these two scenarios could be many things. It could be that in the second scenario, the person had a very supportive family member or friend that truly believed in them, while the person in the first scenario was surrounded by individuals that had a similar worldview to them. It could be that in the second scenario, the person utilized a specific talent, and had a clear purpose which motivated them despite all the hardships that they faced. It could be the interaction of both. It is never really straightforward.

It does take a long time to become aware of the many forces that are at work here, especially when we are making a decision. The purpose of this book is to give each of us a place to start, a way to begin uncovering these forces. It is crucial to become aware of our worldviews, as they may be standing in our way without us even recognizing it. The great news is that these worldviews, as well as our values, are changeable: none of them are permanent, and each part of the equation plays and interacts with other parts. These worldviews are neither right nor wrong, but are about how we view and interpret the world. Therefore, we are a constant work in progress, and each experience and person that we meet adds another level of interaction.

Keep in mind that the more interactions we have, the less effect new ones have. The first experiences and people we interact with carry the heaviest weight, and as we add more and more layers, each new layer becomes less influential than the previous ones, unless the nature of the relationship or experience changes. For example, we experience love throughout our life, but each experience of it is different. At the start, we experience the love of a child towards their mother. Then the different forms of love like siblings, friends, mentors and, later, love relationships add to our overall life experiences. The way we handle or interpret love was first taught to us by our caretakers, and this shapes our worldview about love for a very long time.

It is often altered when we find a partner that changes our interpretation of love, either for better or for worse. For example, if our first experience of love from our caretakers was based on conditions ("If you behave well or if you succeed, I will love you,"), this will shape our worldview about love for a long time. Until we meet someone that loves us 'just the way we are', this belief will determine whether we succeed or fail. On the other hand, if we had parents that loved us unconditionally, but in our first experience of romantic love, the individual either cheats on us or betrays our trust, this can shift the perspective of love in our eyes, depending on the intensity of the experience. Similarly, our first experience with romantic love can set the tone for other encounters of romantic love and can, at times, create the feeling of a heavy weight we are forced to carry. Our worldviews are the accumulation of all the experiences, people, and values that we have encountered.

## ***Reflection***

Reflect on some of your own personal worldviews.

• How is it that you see the world?

• What are some of your core beliefs about how the world works?

## Values, Worldviews And Their Interaction.

What is the difference between worldviews and values? Values are what we place importance on and what we give our time to. Worldviews are a set of assumptions about how the world works, the color in which we choose to shade every interaction that we make. Therefore, whereas values pinpoint specific characteristics or ideals that we strive towards, worldviews are more generalized perspectives based on our values.

As an example of how worldviews and values can interact with one another, let's look at Andrew. Andrew valued luxury items, because as he grew up, his parents used to judge people by what they wore and how they presented themselves. They would look upon others with disdain if they did not match a certain look or type. Therefore, Andrew adopted his parents' values of 'looking good' and dressing well. At times, the voices in his head would argue about trying to save money, as his budget was tight sometimes, but the 'need to impress' was also important to him. His worldview was something along the lines of: "Expensive and fancy clothes are signs of a better person."

Whether he was aware of this worldview or not, every argument between his internal voices contained a hint of it. If he was going out shopping and he went directly to the brand names, the values from his parents would say: "Buy a brand name; they are always better." His worldview voice would say: "Brand names are higher quality, so I will look better." Then his bank account would say: "If you buy another brand suit, you will not have enough money to eat." Then his DNA and survival instinct voice would say: "I need to have enough money to eat." Sometimes the worldview and values beat out the other two voices, and that is why we see individuals in debt – those who drive the $100,000 cars, but can barely afford to put food on the table.

## Filter Three: Our Hungers

While our values and worldviews are formed due to the interaction of our experiences and the people we meet, our hungers can include interactions that never occurred. These are needs that were never fulfilled. When these kinds of interactions fail to occur, we seek them almost religiously as we grow older.

Let us return to the example of Amber the perfectionist. Remember that as she was growing up, Amber never really felt loved or appreciated. The only time that she praised or got the attention she needed from her parents was when she succeeded in competitions or got high grades. She then went to the extreme of perfectionism because that was the only way she knew to get attention from the people that mattered to her at the time. This was her way of striving to fulfill her unmet needs, which were attention and affection. However, her actions came with a price, because to succeed the way she wanted to, she had to detach herself from future interactions with others. For her, all that mattered was success and being at the top of her game. She did not realize until it was too late that all this need for success did not come from a place of purpose and love; it came from a place of hunger and need, a need to be seen, and a need to get the attention that she so desperately sought.

I must reiterate once again that our values, worldviews, and hungers are not voices on their own. They are the fixed patterns that occur, the filters through which we see future interactions. They are formed after an accumulation of interactions, and they are grounded in those experiences, people that founded those needs, and viewpoints.

## What Are Hungers?

What is the first thing that comes to our mind when we think about the word 'hungry'? We think of a growling stomach, a stomach that is relatively empty, and perhaps a stomach that has not been fed for hours. **Hungers are the missing psychological needs that we crave, and that, at times, drive us.** They contribute to another filter of the voices. However, we must first understand some of our basic needs, to understand what – exactly – we are hungry for.

**Survival, Safety, and Security.** From the moment we are born, we all have basic needs — as we saw in Maslow's *Hierarchy of Needs* in the Introduction. There are many human needs, but in my opinion, there are a few needs that cannot be ignored. These are survival, safety, and security. If we do not feel that we are capable of surviving, or that we have the food, shelter, etc., that we need, then there will be no room for us to think of anything else. When this need is unmet, we may resort to stealing, or even killing, for our innate need to survive is extremely strong.

**Being Touched and Receiving Attention.** It is proven that when a baby is carried and touched it helps with their growth and development. In general, humans require human touch and human contact, and it makes us happier. A famous experiment conducted in the 1950s by psychologist Harry Harlow showed the need for love in mammals. When the experiment was conducted on a baby monkey, there were two machines placed in the cage with it. One was covered in warm and soft cloth, but the other machine monkey was not soft. It was cold and wiry, but dispensed milk for the baby monkey. The experiment showed that the baby monkey kept hugging the soft monkey, and only went to the rough one when it needed food. It chose to stay near the monkey that it felt warmth towards, not necessarily the one that fed it. Because of this, the need for touch and warmth is recognized even in animals.

**Acceptance and Belonging.** Humans are social creatures, and our need to belong and be part of a group is innate. When we become isolated, or have little to no human connection, this may transform into a hunger and individuals may go to extremes just to be part of a group. Think of individuals in a high school. Each teenager wants to be part of a group. They are either one of the 'popular' kids or the 'jockeys' or the 'nerds'. There are so many labels we create because of our innate desire to belong and to be part of something greater than ourselves.

Consider why football/soccer fans get so invested in their sport? It is not about someone kicking a ball into a goal. It becomes about a sense of belonging, a feeling that when my team wins, I am a winner too! There have been many news stories about mobs that get violent during sports events, because we take our sense of belonging so seriously.

**Freedom and Being True to Oneself.** Alongside acceptance and belonging, we have the need to be true to ourselves, to not try and be someone else, and to experience the freedom that accompanies this. We often live in very restrictive societies where we are told what we must do and how we should act, and there are many actions that are not permissible. Our entire sense of being is contingent on the 'Dos' and 'Don'ts' that are set out by others. We will constantly have a need to break free, and some of us will respond so strongly to this need that we will take every opportunity to rebel. For example, if we were raised in a family that was extremely constrictive, the moment we are able to venture out on our own, we may go to the other extreme just to revel in a sense of freedom. With too much restriction in our lives, we will never truly know what we like or dislike. The instant that we are given freedom, we will, at first, most likely abuse it just to figure out parts of who we really are.

**Grieving Our Losses.** At times, we undergo the loss of someone or something dear to us, a job, or even the image of a person that we thought was real. All of these things can be considered losses, and the right amount of time is needed for the grieving process to ensue. As discussed earlier, if we are not allowed to properly grieve, this can result in suppression and it will eventually show up in other facets of our life. We will start to develop a hunger centered on it, without even realizing. We may not be able to let go of the loss, and eventually our attachment to it will become maladaptive.

When we lose a loved one, some of us may be unable to enter the room that the individual once slept in, sometimes for years after the tragedy occurs. We may find that we can no longer sleep in the bed that we shared with our now deceased spouse. This can indicate either that we were not given the opportunity to grieve, or that we are denying the fact that this person is lost to us. This is because the people who influence us are so significant and important in our lives.

**Growth and Sense of Accomplishment.** A vital need for human beings is a sense of growth and accomplishment. We must all grow and move forward. If our environment does not allow us to grow, this need will evolve into a hunger and may manifest in destructive ways.

For example, when we stay in the same job for over 20 years and there is no room for learning or improvement, we may feel like we are in a cage day after day, doing the same thing. If we do not find chances to grow, we feel something is missing, that our life has stagnated and is not leading to anything better. Humans have a need to push the limits, otherwise we would have been satisfied with hunting for food the way our ancestors used to do, instead of innovating and improving ourselves.

**All We Need is Love!** This is the central need that we all have as human beings, one that opens the door and grants us the ability to reach the best version of ourselves. Once we have secured this need, it will be a source of strength. When it is missing, we seek it, sometimes in the most unconventional fashions. Love has many faces. The love we receive from our parents, from our partners, and from our children all represent different facets of love. Each one adds another layer, but at the core, having love in our lives, whichever facet of it is present, is a vital necessity.

If it is missing, we may seek it in destructive ways. We may stay in a relationship where the other individual does not respect or love us, because in the end we do not really know what love is, and nor do we feel it towards ourselves. We may seek the affection of others desperately, and become a doormat in some instances, because the hunger becomes too severe and we feel that we need it greatly, even at the cost of our self-respect. Love is an essential need that we all seek to fulfill.

All of these forms of 'love' can, at times, be an over-compensation for a lack of secure attachment and love we felt as children. The need for love becomes a hunger, and so later when we seek love, we seek it in abundance, in a distorted or perhaps unrealistic way. It is important to become aware of these needs, and, if they were unmet in our lives, become conscious of how they transform into hungers, and what we can do to not give them power over us.

When regular needs are not met, they manifest into hungers, and this can become dangerous, because then the need is amplified. When our needs are not met in healthy and/or productive ways, we go about satisfying these needs in potentially harmful or questionable ways. When our hungers take over we may seek to satisfy our needs through escapist behaviors. These include over-pursuing the need or numbing the pain that accompanies the need, through drugs, excessive drinking, sex (in an excessive or compulsive manner), excessive video gaming, and other forms of distractions.

Let's consider an example where the parents were emotionally and physically unavailable for their child, perhaps because they traveled a lot or worked all the time. This could result in the child feeling a lack of emotional security. If, every time the parents returned from long periods of time away, they brought with them gifts, toys, and clothes, the child might have started to believe that affection is shown through material gain. Perhaps later in life, they will then seek material gain continually because, on an unconscious level, they associate it with parental care and presence. They then become excessive shoppers and spend lots of money on extravagant things, in order to be given the attention that they lacked when they were a child, and may still be lacking. For them, it becomes a hunger that they need to satisfy.

If the hungers are very severe, they can overpower even our values and the other voices in our lives. For example, if our hunger for attention is extremely strong, those of us who seek fame and fortune may do so through illegal means, just because we have an incessant need to quiet that voice. The hunger that drives us will overpower our sense of right and wrong. Having opted to satiate our hunger through illegal means, we may, at the beginning, struggle to come to terms with acting illegally. However, we will eventually quiet the objecting voices and justify our actions. Our values will slowly shift to match our hungers. Hungers are powerful, and therefore it is important for us to recognize them.

Let us look at an example that shows how all three of the filters interact with one another. Bob grew up in a family with 7 sisters and 4 brothers. It was a large family, and within this family, sharing with one another was a value that was inherited by all. As Bob had so many older siblings, hand-me-downs were a common thing, and getting new toys was something of a rarity for him. Due to the fact that his living space was occupied by so many others, personal boundaries were not really recognized, as there was literally no space for individual occupations. Bob would willingly share his food with his friends at school, and sometimes help himself to their things without asking.

Some of Bob's values included the importance of family and sharing. His worldviews were: 'Life is a team effort', and 'Your identity is part of the whole; if the group fails, so do you'. His hungers included both his sense of independence and freedom. Although he enjoyed the support that he received from his family members, he always had a part of him that sought freedom. The voices in his head always supported his values, but at the same time, his friends and people outside of his family made him recognize the possibility of independence.

All of these forces interact, and during such collisions, we place importance on some voices over others.

Hungers are a very important filter to take into consideration, because if they are strong enough, they can control every aspect of the other voices. Some people, when their needs are completely neglected, cannot see past their hungers, because the hungers surpass all of their values and voices.

**When our psychological hungers become very strong within us, they can become so loud that nothing else will be heard, and nothing else will matter.**

## *__Reflection__*

I ask that you take some time to go over the list of needs once more. Afterwards, think about what hungers you may have.  List your thoughts. Be honest and truthful, and remember that only you will have access to your answers.

After you have listed them, take some time to consider the following questions:

- What needs do you believe you have secured?

- What needs do you feel you are lacking?

- Can you think of a time in your life when you felt the urge to seek something out? Is it possible that this urge was the result of a hunger?

- Are there any dysfunctional habits in your life? Could the reason behind them be a hunger?

- Which of the hungers you have identified do you believe you need to address?

- What can you do to fulfill those needs in a healthy and functional way?

Now that you have read all of the above, take some time to honestly revisit your reflections of your values, your worldviews, and your hungers. When you are ready, fill in the table below with what you believe are your filters. Put both the negative and the positive, labeling them accordingly.

| Values | | Worldviews | | Hunger |
| --- | --- | --- | --- | --- |
| Aspired | Current | Positive | Negative | |
| | | | | |
| | | | | |
| | | | | |
| | | | | |
| | | | | |
| | | | | |
| | | | | |
| | | | | |

*CHAPTER FIVE*

# OUR PURPOSE IS OUR KEY

**One voice to rule them all. That is purpose.** Often, we get so encapsulated and confused by the many voices in our heads that we forget the one that actually counts, the one that takes into consideration our passions and what we truly love. You need to create your own voice, one that allows space for all the other voices, but filters them based on how they benefit your overall purpose.

This voice should be the driving force of the rest. This is the voice that we sometimes neglect, or place on the back burner, as other voices are introduced and become strong forces in our lives. Your purpose can be considered a point of reference, a way of life that you would like to adopt. It is your authentic self, and it brings peace and joy to your overall interactions.

# VOICE OF PURPOSE

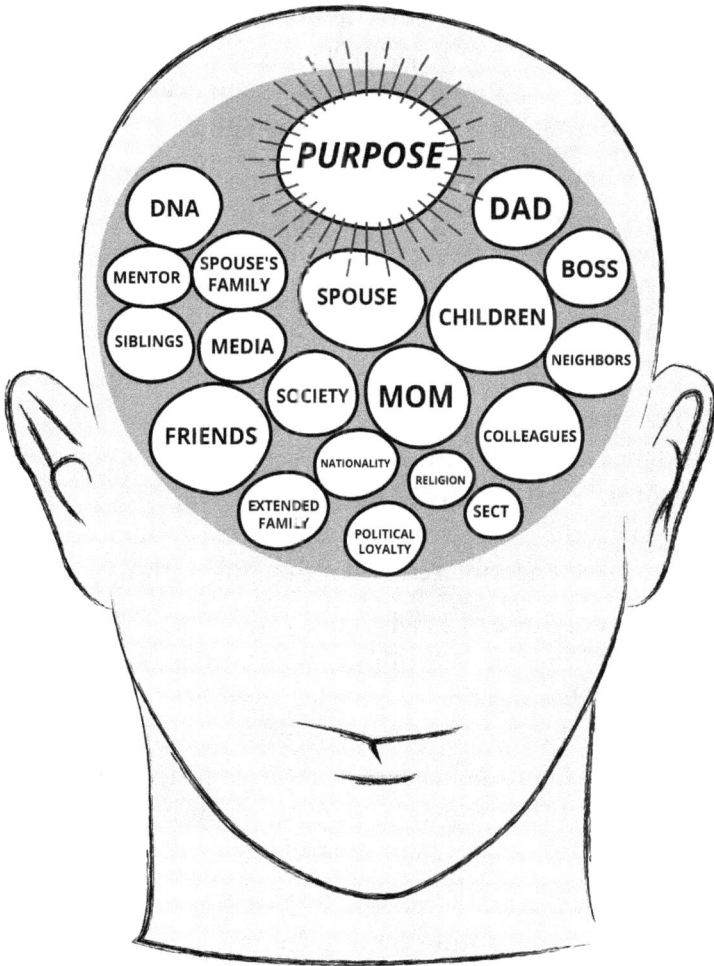

In all of history, space, and time, the person that you see when you look in the mirror – this face, these eyes, the way you smile – will never be repeated. **There will never be another YOU** that is made up of exactly the same voices, from your DNA, to the people you connect with, to the experiences you have, and the values, worldviews, and hungers that you discover in yourself. Even identical twins still have experiences that make them venture down different paths, and even their fingerprints are different.

Each of us is made in a very unique and different way. Some of us get excited when we enter a math classroom and we see each math problem as a riddle that we can crack open and solve. Others of us, on entering the same classroom, would see these equations as gibberish, unintelligible babble that we have to memorize and utilize!

For some of us, music comes easily. We "have rhythm", and dance to beats with fluidity. Others of us, when we attempt to "bust a move", look like 'bobble heads' instead, and — beware — toe-stepping, eye-poking and accidental slaps may be encountered when dancing with us!

There are those of us who get enraptured by the written word, and long for late nights, cups of cocoa, and good books. We dream of a world filled with poetic prose and philosophical debates. Yet others of us cannot stand the written word, and believe in "a cigar, is just a cigar" type thinking. In other words, we do not want or like hidden meaning! Give us clear cut answers!

All these illustrate the idea that we are all unique, and that we are created and function in very different ways.

Our uniqueness, in some respects, is very much related to our DNA. If someone has a particular talent, a deeper voice, a certain look, or perhaps a particular body type or shape, they may be better suited for certain activities. For example, basketball players are often tall as it is easier for them to reach the basket; they have an advantage over other players that are shorter. There are features and qualities that come encoded in our DNA that make us more suited for certain things.

## *Reflection*

You, like all of us, have something that puts a smile on your face, that makes you feel ike you are floating on air, and that makes your heart sing. That is your purpose. To start figuring out what your purpose is consider for a moment:

- What do you love to do?

- What makes your heart sing?

- What keeps you moving forward, no matter how hard things get?

Reflect on the experiences in your life where you felt blissful, happy, and joyful. Wher you felt that nothing else mattered — that you could take on the world.

- What were you doing at that time?

## Where Does Purpose Come In?

Remember that each living organism is built to survive, but this is not enough for humans. Our ultimate purpose is survival and growth. Additionally, each of us has a unique purpose that aids in the ultimate purpose of survival and growth. *Your purpose* **is placing your uniqueness in the service of others.** This does not have to be a selfless act, where you devote your lives to others at a personal cost which robs you of joy.

Each and every one of us has a special purpose that moves and dances beneath the surface. It is something that brings you to life, that you enjoy doing. Purpose, at the end of the day, is the combination of your passion and what you are really good at, as well as something that serves others.

Think of your unique qualities as an inventory list. Combine that list with something that can add value, and then combine it again with what you love to do.

For example, let us consider someone who has a beautiful voice, which we consider to be a unique quality of this particular person. If they just end up singing in the shower, nobody benefits from their talent, no one gets to appreciate the beauty of their voice. But if this person loves to sing, and feels that they come alive when they sing, why not share it with the rest of the world? There are many ways this person can share their beautiful voice, they do not have to pursue singing professionally. For instance, they could make it a form of contribution to the community, occasionally volunteering their time to make others happy (frequently singing at a nursing home, hospital, or a daycare center). Sharing your talents will not only bring joy to others, but also to yourself. It is a two-way enriching interaction.

Maya Angelou said, "I believe that everyone is born with talent", and she goes on to explain that it is how we use it that makes the difference. For some, their uniqueness includes a talent for painting, and their purpose may be to paint murals around the city, in order to add more beauty to life. Another person might have a unique talent in cooking, and this person will become a chef, letting everyone enjoy his/her creations. Others still may not have a specific talent that is obvious, but they enjoy certain tasks, and when they are doing these things, they feel that time flies by.

Therefore, it is key to **reflect** on and think back to the activities that we enjoy. At times we can look to our childhood to get hints about what we love doing by what experiences still stand out to us as particularly memorable. A child may have the strangest hobbies or interests, but developing these can actually result in something worthwhile.

Mozart is an example of an individual who followed his purpose when he discovered that he had a specific talent. He was composing music at five years old! His raw talent was undeniable, but his experience of constant practice and perfecting this talent was also something that was needed. Fortunately, his father was a music teacher, who supported Mozart and potentially became an internal voice that encouraged him to feed the talent that he already clearly had.

It is how we **nurture and develop** the talents that we are given that make them come to life – or not. Similarly, Oprah Winfrey is an example of someone who had a talent for talking and connecting with others. She ended up producing one of the most famous talk shows in the world. She recognized her talent, and created opportunities to share it with the world. It could have been the internal voices that Oprah had which encouraged her to not give up, but it could have also been the adverse experiences that she had, which helped her to connect with others who suffered the same misfortunes that she did. Her experiences made her more down-to-earth and approachable, and she became a symbol of someone who was strong enough to speak up. Both she and Mozart were talented in very different and unique ways, and both were able to take advantage of and leverage their talents for the benefit of others.

Sometimes it is not even a particular talent that ends up becoming our purpose, but an experience that makes us see the world differently. For example, many individuals who have become disabled in some way have taken their adversity and used it to move forward.

The story of Paul Wood is an example of a person activating self-transformation after experiencing adversity. As a teenager, he got addicted to drugs after his mother got really sick. He ended up murdering his drug dealer at the age of 18, claiming that the 42-year-old man made unwanted sexual advances towards him. He was sentenced to 11 years in prison, but during those 11 years in prison, he did not allow that experience to keep him down or block his growth as a person. With the support of his father and teachers, he was still able to graduate from college, and even ended up leaving prison half-way through his PhD in Psychology. At the end of his prison sentence, he felt freer than he ever did before, and he had the willpower to help others change their lives for the better.

The adversity that he had undergone did not stand in his way. It made him stronger, and it made him want to come out fighting. He had the time and the strength to move past his situation, and he devoted his time to studying and improving himself. During this time, he had the support of various mentors and family members who pushed him to move past the situation he was in. He had his father, who was a continual support, as well as professors who were willing to come and supervise him within the prison. He began to realize that prison was not the end of the road for him. When his internal voices supported his purpose and he actually adhered to it, he was able to make the decision to get better and to not fall into the regular self-defeating and destructive patterns which many other prison inmates succumb to.

Another famous story of an individual who was able to find purpose through adversity was Dashrath Manjhi, also known as "mountain man". Manjhi, after losing his wife on a dangerous mountain route, ended up picking up a hammer and starting to chip away at the mountain in order to make a safer route. For many years, people thought he was crazy, wondering how he could take up such a challenge all by himself. He devoted the rest of his life to it, waking up each morning, slowly chipping away at the mountain side. He was able to do something that no one thought one man could do alone: he was able to dig through a mountain. This was only possible because of his sheer will and persistence. He was able to create a safe route, reduced the traveling time greatly, and eventually a road was actually built. He created a much safer option for those walking that path, and he did it with just his two hands and a hammer.

Some people will fall when they encounter a tragedy such as losing a loved one; others will stand up and make the most out of their situation. The death of his wife could have potentially made her voice stronger in his head. It could also have been guilt which drove him, as she was bringing him lunch when she fell. Perhaps it was a mixture of voices that got him to pick up that hammer, but he would not have persisted for that long had he not had a stronger force driving him. If he had only been fueled by guilt or grief, he might have stopped a quarter of the way in, but he kept going. Perhaps he realized the trouble that other people were going through, and wanted to help. Sometimes what pushes us towards our purpose is not a particular skill or talent, but an experience that shakes us, that wakes us up and makes us want to do better, and to be better.

Therefore, the voice of purpose can emerge through certain talents that are part of our DNA, which are encouraged through the experiences that we have, and the internal voices that either support or suppress these talents. Alternatively, this emergence can come about through the experiences that have taught us lessons and shifted our values or worldviews. However our voice of purpose emerges, the key differentiation when we are listening to it is that it comes from deep within. Those of us that follow our purpose reach a place where we experience a sense of peace and satisfaction.

**The last element of purpose is placing it in the service of others.** This does not necessarily mean we must devote our lives to a cause. It could just mean bringing art and beauty into the lives of others. It is about sharing the most genuine parts of ourselves, the core of our beings, the bits that are truly alive and passionate. When we are doing something that we love, we tend to light up, and that affects all the people around us as well.

## *Reflection*

Each and every one of us has something unique to offer. Take some time to think about what you bring to the table.

- What gifts, talents, interests, etc., do you have?
- How can you put this uniqueness in the service of others?

Another way to think about it:

- What makes you happy and can elevate other peoples' lives?

In a study in 2006, Jorge Moll and his colleagues conducted a brain imaging test, and found that when the subjects chose to donate to charitable causes, (helping others and contributing to their well-being), this activated their mesolimbic system, which triggers the part of the brain which transmits a sense of blessing and reward. This means

97

that helping others out automatically makes us feel good. Helping others is wired into our DNA, because we receive positive benefits from it, whether we realize it or not.

Following a purpose that serves others as well as ourselves can have endless benefits. It is not just a selfless act, but improves the life of the giver too, because we feel good and happy about it. Remember also that doing a good deed can encourage others to follow suit. We may actually start a chain reaction of good deeds.

## *Reflection*

In a 2010 study by Simone Schnall, Jean Roper, and Daniel M.T. Fessler, it was discovered that watching clips of other people acting pro-socially could encourage the subject of the 2 experiments to volunteer for tasks that they would not be compensated for. The conclusion of this is that, seeing others act in a pro-social way can actually encourage those watching to go out and to do something selfless themselves.

• Recall a time when you personally witnessed someone do something for others. Did this motivate you to follow in their footsteps? If yes, what did you do? How did it make you feel?

• Recall a time when you yourself did something to help another person out. Did this encourage people to take the time and do something for others?

All of the other voices discussed within this book (excluding DNA) come from an outside source. Purpose is not meant to come from something external which we have internalized. **Purpose is something that comes from**

**within that we choose to externalize.** Everything else, up until now, discussed what the world was giving to us, through individuals that we encountered, culture, experiences, etc. In contrast, purpose is something that comes from within us, a talent, an interest, something that we love, and that we choose to build upon and offer to others. We can each think of ourselves as individual puzzle pieces in the grander plan of the world. We each have a message to send, something to give back, which adds value to the collective and gets passed down.

## *Reflection*

I want you to imagine what the best version of yourself is.

To start off, take a moment to consider your created filters:

- Think about your aspired values.
- Think about your positive worldviews.
- Think about your positive self-beliefs.
- Think about the positive things the people in your life say about you.
- Imagine shedding all those unwanted values, worldviews, and hungers.

Next, I want you to gather the information from your reflections on your purpose and what you have to offer.

Now combine that information with the information on your created filters. Keep it in mind and ask yourself the following question:

- Who is the authentic you? The "hero" you?

Take a moment to describe the authentic version of yourself.

## Clarifying What Purpose Is

There are a few things about purpose that must be made clear, however. **Purpose is a life-long goal that individuals should work towards.** Purpose does not end, no matter what stage we are in. For example, let us think about the situation of an individual whose purpose is to heal others, and who has chosen a profession as a doctor. If they stop being a doctor, this does not mean that their purpose ends. There are many ways to 'heal' people. Furthermore, purpose is not limited to a role or profession. We could be an accountant, but our purpose could be related to painting, which for us is a hobby. Many people believe that if they have found their purpose, there is an ending to it or there is a point where they can stop fulfilling it, but it never really ends.

Additionally, the process is **not time-sensitive.** You can find your purpose at any age. There were many famous artists, writers and/or actors that did not start pursuing their careers until later on in their lives, or individuals that either did not know what they wanted to devote their life to until their 40s, 50s or even well into their 70s and 80s. For example, Adeline De Walt Reynolds made her film debut at the age of 79. Daniel Defoe decided to write fiction and wrote Robinson Crusoe when he was around 59 years old. Anna Mary Robertson (a.k.a. "Grandma Moses") pursued her dream to be a painter at around the age of 76; she went on to make over 1,500 paintings in her lifetime and receive wide acclaim for her work. Julia Child did not take steps to learn cooking till she was 36 years of age, and it was not till she was 51 years old that she had her own TV cooking show. Millard Kaufman, a novelist and screenwriter, wrote his first novel at the age of 90. There are many more examples of famous people that were able to reach their purpose, so what is stopping us? It is never too late to discover what our purpose is.

Purpose is **not about money or fame.** Sometimes those things are attached to finding our purpose, but they should not be our sole focus. If we focus on providing others with value and contributing to their survival and growth, naturally they will be drawn to us and may be a source of money, fame, or both. However, purpose should be something that makes us come alive, something that we would do even if nobody was watching. It is something that lights us up and puts a spark in our eyes. When we have discovered our purpose, we will know it because when we are actually fulfilling it, and although it is not easy, it will feel like time is passing by very fast. It is something that we genuinely enjoy from the bottom of our hearts.

**Purpose comes from the most authentic and real part of who you are.** That is why, if your voice of purpose is not strong and it is lingering in the background, it is time to bring it to the front and recognize its importance.

"Let yourself be silently drawn by the strange pull of what you really love."

*– Rumi*

# DEFAULT SETTING

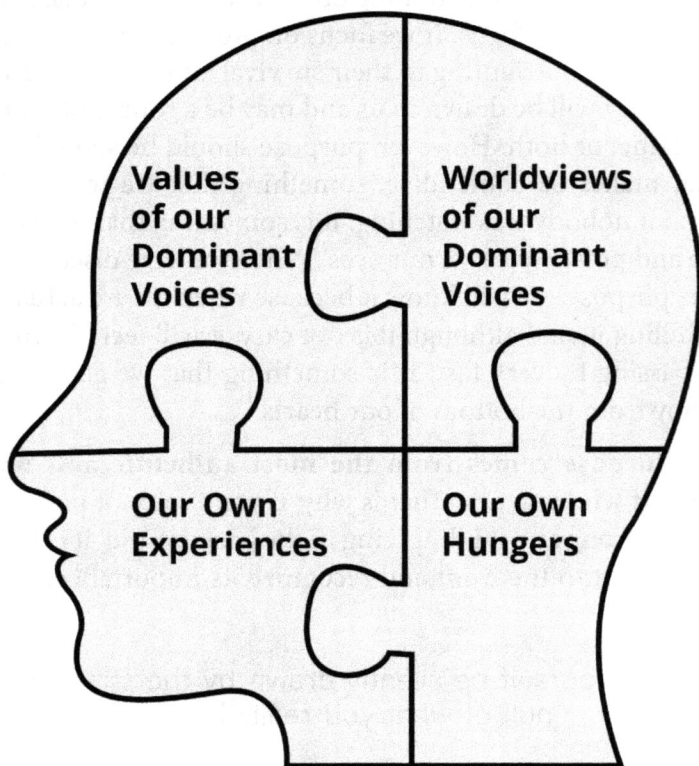

Values of our Dominant Voices

Worldviews of our Dominant Voices

Our Own Experiences

Our Own Hungers

# Decisions: Ours or Not?

It is important to recognize all of these above layers because they constitute our unique **"default setting."** The way we currently function is unconsciously dictated by the layers of voices, and their interactions with our experiences and our various filters. This default setting affects the way we think, feel, act, and make decisions. It forms our patterns, which dictate our behavior and character, and therefore shape our future, most of the time without us even realizing it. The voices affect all our major decisions. If we want to take a more philosophical perspective on it, we are the way we are because of the decisions that we have made. So, in one way or another, each of us is the accumulation of the decisions that we make on a daily basis.

Every time we make decisions, all these voices come into play, including the voice of our DNA, the voices of people in our heads, and the voice of our purpose, interacting with our experiences and creating our values, worldviews, and hungers.

Each one of these voices pulls us in a different direction and forms alliances with other voices. The alliance which is the strongest, or the "loudest", ends up winning and pulling us in the direction it wants. All of these processes are happening on a subconscious level. We are making decisions without really knowing where the actual pull comes from. Most of us are **unaware** of the voices that direct our lives, so we think that we are making the decisions, but the reality is that all these various needs and influencers are making the decisions for us. We can argue that these voices are us, which is true to a certain degree, but being aware of them gives us the choice of whether to follow a particular voice or not. The ability to make conscious decisions is a very powerful tool.

*CHAPTER SIX*

# MAKING CONSCIOUS DECISIONS

There are very rare occasions when the decisions we make are actually our own. This occurs when the following steps are taken, and we 'wake up':

**1- Knowing who we are and understanding all the voices that form us.**

It is important that we understand all the different voices that are a part of us, and the many layers that accompany them. Think of this like an excavation. We need to dig down and understand all the various layers of ourselves and differentiate between them. Once we have done this, we can better recognize when our DNA is playing its part and when it's standing in the way, and we will begin to understand what our values and worldviews truly are, and how they sway us from one direction to the other. We will see how these influences and experiences have made us more inclined to make certain choices. Once we know and understand these different elements, we can stop the patterns that are no longer working for us.

Let's revisit the example of Amber, the perfectionist. If she had a better understanding of her perfectionism, perhaps she could have seen that, in the past, it had benefitted her — it protected her from the her parents' disapproval. However, she would also have recognized that in her current reality and at her job, it was hindering her performance. Her ability to identify the pattern and whether it was necessary could be life-changing.

All of the different aspects affect us in more ways than we can fathom, but with awareness of the urges and hungers we have, our various worldviews and values, we can start to either re-affirm them or begin to change them. At the end of the day, with awareness comes some semblance of control, and the ability to start making our own conscious decisions. For example, imagine that we are in a relationship, and consistently shut ourselves off during an argument. We do this because it is a way of protecting ourselves from pain (perhaps from prior experience), it will take recognition of this pattern to stop it in its tracks. With awareness comes power – but that is only the first step!

### 2- Having a clear purpose that gives us peace and joy.

As stated before, purpose is one of the voices, but if the other voices are too strong, it may get lost in the mix. It is important to become very aware of your purpose so that it can guide you on all of your decisions. Remember that when you are following your purpose, you are following the most authentic part of yourself. It is the part that comes alive, not the one that is clogged up by fears, insecurities, or hungers. It is your truest potential that wants to come out, and work its magic!

It is essential that we stay aware of our purpose and let it speak, because most of the time our experiences, the people around us, etc., will push us away from our purpose. They will try to get us to fulfill their own needs, hungers, etc. For example, imagine we have a partner or a friend that is too controlling but means the world to us. When, time and time again, they show us that what they say is correct and that our way ends up getting us into trouble, we may start to distrust our own way of seeing things. At some point we may even distrust that our purpose is truly the right way. We may eventually just follow this person blindly, or obey the internalized version of their voice, without taking into consideration what we ourselves want. They might convince us to pursue a college major or career path that is more practical, as it will be safer and provide a steady income. Although we want to pursue something more risky that fulfills a passion, painting for example, we may hesitate if our previous experiences have left us penniless and painting on a street corner. We may start to quiet the voice that loves to paint, we may take on that "comfortable and safe" job and forget who we originally wanted to be in the process. Purpose does not have to be the only thing that is important in our lives, but we need to recognize it, otherwise resentment will follow, because our hearts and souls are unfulfilled.

**3- Having the courage and the awareness to listen to all the voices, but making decisions based on our purpose** to ensure the best outcome for our survival and growth, even if it means disappointing some of the louder voices.

At the end of the day, none of the above steps will be possible if we do not have the courage to sometimes disappoint the dominant voices. Most of the time, we go through our lives listening to just one voice, and we are so unaware that we forget our own. When we start to recognize that we are doing things for someone else or for another voice, it feels risky to back away from something that seemed so familiar, but it is very important to realize that we were doing it unconsciously.

When we become **aware**, it is still tricky, but if we are able to find a clear purpose and a clear direction, then disappointing the important people in our lives becomes a little less scary. In fact, to a certain degree, it can be empowering, because we will have gained awareness, and we will also have a clear sense of what we want.

We will know ourselves, and understand what makes us tick, not what others think of us, or want us to be. We will live our lives based on our own perception of ourselves, not on the opinions of others. Instead of seeing ourselves through the lens of others' voices, our own experiences, and our unfulfilled needs, we can step back, recognize all those layers and aspects of ourselves and say: 'Well this is what I want to follow', or 'This is the path that I want to take', or 'I recognize that I have these certain needs that may not go away, but perhaps giving into them in the wrong ways will not satisfy or fulfill them".

Give yourself the time and patience to be able to recognize these things and get yourself to the point where you say: "I want something more than this".

It is time to wipe away everything else and hold a magnifying glass up to ourselves. We have the **ability** to become whatever we choose to become. With awareness, we are no longer slaves to the voices within us. In fact, **WE ARE NOT OUR VOICES.** How freeing this notion can be! They will always be a part of us, but at least now we have the courage to say no, we have the courage to back away when we need to, and we may even have the courage to disappoint some of the voices that we never thought we would be able to ignore.

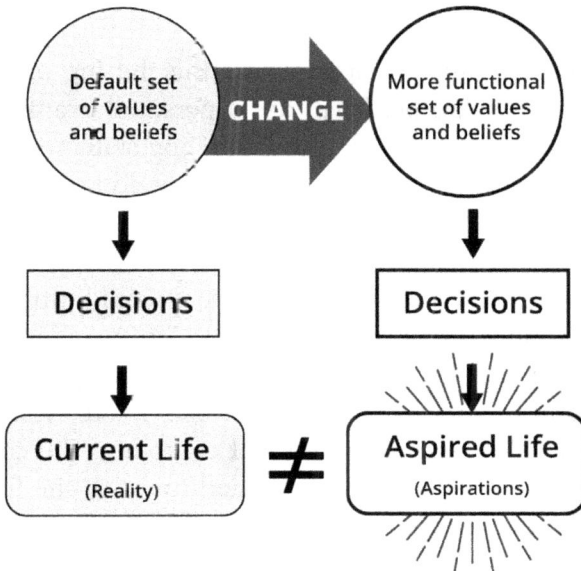

## *Reflection*

Having read this new information go back to the table of influencers and voices in chapter three. Look over the list, and make sure you have included all the influencers that come to mind. Now reexamine these questions:

- Which voices are holding you back?

- Which voices are encouraging you?

- Which voices do feel you need to challenge?

- Which voices do you believe you have to say no to?

> "What a liberation to realize that the 'voice in my head' is not who I am. Who am I then? The one who sees that."
>
> *– Eckhart Tolle*

To draw out just how frustrating the tug of war between voices can be, I will use a personal example to illustrate what I meant by the surprising statement I made at the beginning of this book – that we do not necessarily make our own decisions. Ever since I was a child, the topic of leadership has always fascinated me. I would not just read books that discussed this topic; I would inhale them! It made me feel alive and curious. As I grew older, my love for leadership got mixed with a variety of obligations. At one point in my life, I had a decision to make. At the time, I was a CEO of an international company. The compensation was great, and this provided me with the financial stability that I needed to support my family, but I could not honestly say that I was happy.

During my weekends and personal time, I was running my own think tank; The Cambridge Institute for Global Leadership, an institute devoted to research, through which we provide workshops about leadership, purpose, and authority. When I gave those workshops, I truly felt alive. It was when I was really breathing! The problem was that my duties as a CEO were conflicting with the time and effort that I wanted to put into my company. I had to make a decision. Should I leave the position, and focus on what truly made me happy? Or stay in the cushy job that would give me more than I could need?

I chose to leave, and that was the first time in my entire life that I actually made my own decision. The reason that I was staying in the cushy job was because of the various voices in my head. My purpose, my authentic self, convinced me to leave the corporate world and dedicate my life to spreading the concept of purposeful leadership.

There were many other voices however, that were against this decision. Some voices were those of friends who said: "It would be foolish at the peak of your career, your professional level, in your mid-40s, to leave a fantastically paying job and position as a CEO, with all its benefits, including prestige, power, and ego." Another set of voices said: "You have a very well-paying job, and it would be asking for trouble to throw yourself into the unknown to initiate a new path." The voices of my hungers and values were saying: "Will this succeed or not? I have children. What about their future?" There were other voices that were trying to negotiate the middle ground: "How about you work for a few more years? Then you can do the leadership thing after some time, after you finish and retire from the corporate world."

There were other voices that were supporting me, saying: "No! Do it! You only live once!" The various voices were fighting, voices ranging from family and friends to even wider circles of social acquaintances. Even after I took the decision, the voices didn't calm down. They were still there, for example, every time there were obstacles in pursuing the new path. It was not smooth. The insecurities would continually resurface and the following voices would pop up: "I told you that it was not going to be easy, and you have a family, etc. How can you not make their security your priority? Forget your dreams! You are not single; you have duties and responsibilities!" On the other hand, the voices that were positive would say: "Don't worry, it is going to be tough for a bit, but then it will open up slowly, and that is normal."

The negative voices started to feed into the insecurities that I had, and at one point, there was too much economic instability in the country, so I had to compromise on my purpose, and negotiate with myself. I went back half a step and joined the corporate world again, while trying as hard as I could to maintain the Cambridge Institute. The negative voices about my decision had been so strong that I felt I had to listen to them, although I still wanted to maintain my research interest in purposeful leadership.

After things had calmed down, I decided to start listening to my authentic voice again and, after a few years, I re-evaluated my original decision, having quieted the voices of resistance, and secured the resources to fulfill my financial obligations towards my family. It was then that I was able to follow my authentic voice. Although many voices still argued that I should postpone the decision until after retirement, I took that step.

Voices of doubt, no matter how sure we are about our decision, will follow us – but in the end, it is we who must decide which ones to listen to.

I stuck to my purpose and felt that it was necessary to take that step, although the voices against the decision never really quieted fully. I was able to make the decision when I: 1) recognized the voices, 2) had clarity of purpose and 3) had the courage to disappoint the strong and dominant voices and hungers, and to make decisions that were in line with my authentic self and purpose.

The voices, however, do not only show up in times of distress or major decisions. They can also occur at the simplest of times. Let's look at the following examples and let's increase the pressure in each situation!

You are at the regular coffee shop that you go to every Saturday afternoon. You order your cappuccino with skimmed milk and pass a $20 bill to the cashier. When she gives you back your change, you notice to your surprise that she has returned two dollars extra. What do you do? The second that you realize that she gave you extra money, the voices inside your head start to debate in response. Your mother says: "Even if it's just two dollars, you need to return it," and your father says a similar thing. Your hungers say: "I come to this coffee shop all the time, and I always pay so much! What is two dollars?" In the end, because the appeal of two dollars may not be too much for your hungers to cling onto, or the voice of your mother is strong, you end up going back and returning the two dollars.

Let's add a little bit more pressure! Let's say that you are walking on the street and you find a wallet, lying on the sidewalk. You pick up the wallet and you discover that within the wallet there is $100. When this happens, the voices start to battle. Your mother's voice tells you: "I did not raise you to be a thief!", and your father's voice is similar in nature. Your friend's voice may be slightly different: "Take the $100 and drop off the wallet with the identification cards somewhere else. You need the money." Then come the voices of your own hungers or needs: "Come on, I am drowning in bills, living pay check to pay check, this $100 might let me have one fun evening." Once again, this argument comes out, and your choice depends on which voice is stronger – the voice of your mother and your values, or the voice of your empty bank account. The temptation to keep the $100 bill slowly starts to increase – but so does the guilt and the voice of your mother!

Let's now take it one step further! Let's say that you are enjoying a day at the mall and you are having fun. Suddenly, you realize that you are stepping on something. When you look under your shoe, you discover that you have just stumbled upon a diamond ring. The voices are the same, but now they are screaming! Especially your hungers! They are playing on your weaknesses: "Who are you going to return the diamond ring to? You do not even know who it belongs to. What is the likelihood that it will even reach its owner?" Those thoughts start to race in your head. At the same time, your mother's voice is still telling you: "What about the poor soul that lost her ring? She must be devastated."

*The voices push and pull more ferociously depending on the situation. The more there is at stake, the louder they get. Try and put yourself in these situations. What voices would run through your head? Would you return the money or diamond ring? Or would you keep them? Be honest! (Only your voices can hear you!)*

## Final Words

It is crucial to emphasize something. Recognizing the voices and the many layers is not just about ignoring them, or trying to surpass them. It is important to accept that they are parts of us, and that they will remain our constant companions. However, it is also important, in a way, to learn to disconnect from them. They are not our entirety, and they do not need to dictate what we do or how we react. We need to recognize them, be at peace with them, and then – from a place of recognition and peace – decide which one is most important to us and our purpose. **We should choose purpose every time!** We should choose it in spite of the fact that someone may be disappointed, or that people may look at us differently. We should choose it even if our subsequent experiences may not be as pleasant as we would have liked them to be.

When we are thinking of making a decision, we should consider all the elements that play roles in that decision. All of these elements become layers of voices.

**DEAR READER:** Picture yourself at this current moment. Do you see your face? Now imagine this face is divided into hundreds of people, hundreds of experiences that interact within you. They are all a part of you, yet have nothing to do with you.

All these voices and influences are in the background, and, depending on your awareness while you are making the decision, you can choose to place importance on them – or not.

Now, when you next have to make a significant choice, ask yourself:

***Do I have the courage to make my own decision?***

Your answer to this question will change your life!

# MUTING THE VOICE THAT IS HOLDING YOU BACK

At this point, you may have finished reading the text, answered the reflections, and understood the voices that may influence each of your decisions. You may be asking yourself how you can apply this information to become aware of and deal with your voices. In the last part of this book, there is a workbook that will help you map out the main voices in your mind, reflect on your experiences, consider your created filters (hungers, worldviews, values, and beliefs), and reflect on your voice of purpose.

Whenever you wish to address the voices that are holding you back, take some time to look at and go over the steps below. This may help you to put them on mute.

## STEP 1: Who Is The Negative Dominant Voice?

When you feel that something within you is keeping you from living a fulfilled life, try to reflect on what it is that is holding you back. If it is a voice, then ask:

- Whose voice is it?
- What is this voice telling you?

For instance, it could be that you hear a person's voice

telling you that "you are a total failure" or that "the choices you are making will never work". The voice may be so dominant that you have begun to listen to it automatically. You should look for that source of your hesitation — this person's voice — and understand what it is that this voice is saying. Since it represents someone you may be close to, you are probably inclined to believe it.

## STEP 2: Challenge This Voice

Ask yourself whether this voice's statements are factually correct. Examine your past experiences and see if there is any evidence to support it. If there is no solid and credible evidence, consider challenging it. Think about the experiences in your life that contradict or refute what this voice is telling you.

Let's go back to the example in step one. A person's voice is telling you that "you are a total failure" or that "the choices you are making will not work". You should challenge the voice and ask yourself, "Am I a total failure?" "What evidence supports this?" Then think about any evidence that refutes or contradicts it. For instance, consider the fact that you are still alive despite all the challenges that you have faced in your life; that surely means you are not a "total failure". In the case of the second message, consider what the facts behind your decision-making abilities are. You should challenge that voice by looking at your experiences, focusing on ones where your choices worked, and your life was better for it.

If the voice is still dominant in your mind, despite evidence refuting what it is saying, then you are still listening to the voice because of loyalty. In this case, ask yourself whether it is blind loyalty or conscious loyalty.

Blind loyalty means you are following the voice without knowing it, in which case you may need to revisit the first step and become aware of the voice and your loyalty to it. In the other case — conscious loyalty — you are fully aware of the consequences of being loyal to this voice (it is keeping you from living a fulfilled life). In this case, you need to consider if you want to forego your right to live a fulfilling and meaningful life for the sake of that loyalty. If not, then you will need to challenge the voice, even if it is difficult to do so.

## STEP 3: Imagine Muting This Voice

Imagine, in detail, how your life would look if you just pressed the mute button on this voice. Take a moment, close your eyes, and intensely experience the joy and bliss that come with muting this voice and choosing the voices that are more in line with your purpose. Don't just describe them to yourself, but actually experience them. Do you feel better? How would your life change? Would the quality of your life improve?

Now, imagine how your life would look if, instead, you continue listening to this voice, even if it is going against your purpose. Take another moment, close your eyes, and intensely experience the suffering and negative feelings that will come of continuing to listen to this voice and giving up opportunities that will help you grow and live a fulfilling and meaningful life.

Recall any opportunities you have missed out on so far because you have been listening to this voice. Imagine how much better your life will be if you are no longer afraid of chasing new opportunities.

Apply this step to the example above. You will see how freeing it can be. You will be able to chase after new experiences, and you will no longer be afraid of trying new things — ones that refute this person's voice. Imagine what it would feel like not to be held back anymore. Imagine how freeing that would be.

## STEP 4: Mute This Voice

It is time to turn the volume down on this voice. Be aware of and try to listen to all the voices that you are "hearing" at any particular moment. Search hard for your voice of purpose, and any other positive and encouraging voices, which will highlight good experiences and your best attributes. Pull them out of the crowd and focus on them. Listen to them so that they can help push you forward towards your growth and fulfillment. These voices will give you a boost to get you unstuck, and will help you mute the negative dominant voice.

Instead of hearing the cacophony of noise that keeps you at a standstill, covering your ears, you can turn up the music and hear the symphony that is urging you to live the life you deserve.

## STEP 5: Amplify Your Authentic Voice Of Purpose And Other Positive Voices

Unfortunately, it is not as simple as pushing the mute button once. It is a continuous process, especially as the ignored voice will scream even louder to get your attention. It may play on your feelings of guilt or shame to get you to change your mind and shift your loyalty back to it. To avoid this, you will need to keep focusing your attention on your voice of purpose and other positive voices.

Focus on experiences that refute the negative voice, and use them to continuously amplify your voice of purpose and the other positive voices. Constantly surround yourself with other encouraging voices, and work on trying new things and new experiences that are in line with your purpose. With this strategy and a bit of time, the voices that are in line with your purpose will get louder, and will help you keep the discouraging one on mute.

However, you should not always avoid this voice; remember that in some situations, the voice might have valuable input. The difference is that when you mute the limiting voice and amplify your voice of purpose and the positive voices, you are aware of all the voices and can make the right decision.

When you gain awareness of your voice of purpose, you will find that you are more willing to experience things that are in line with your purpose. The voices are highlighting your true capabilities, and allowing you to make the choices you wish to make. With enough effort and experiences, you will be able to mute the limiting voice and amplify your voice of purpose (among other positive voices).

## Note

Muting a discouraging, negative, or damaging voice and turning your attention to more encouraging and positive voices does not mean that you are disloyal, ungrateful, selfish, or a bad person. It is of the utmost importance that you do not allow such thoughts to keep you from muting a limiting voice. In fact, you should never let this voice stop you from living an authentic, fulfilling and meaningful life — it is your legal and divine right.

Do make sure, however, that the voice is actually holding you back. Do not simply quiet a voice so that you can rebel against the person to whom it belongs. If this voice offers you sound input and will help you make a purposeful decision, then it is not limiting you, but benefiting you. Therefore, mute a voice only if doing so will help you move forward and live the life you deserve.

# MUTING THE VOICE THAT IS HOLDING YOU BACK

### Who Is The Negative Dominant Voice?

**1**

- ✓ Whose voice is it?
- ✓ What is this voice "telling you"?

### Challenge This Voice

**2**

- ✓ Ask yourself if what this voice is telling you is factually correct and accurate.
- ✓ Think about the experiences and events in your life that contradict or refute what this voice is telling you.

### Imagine Muting This Voice

**3**

- ✓ Imagine how your life would be if you continue listening to this voice.
- ✓ Now Imagine and feel how your life would look like if you just press the mute button. Think of all the experiences and opportunities that you would have if this voice was not holding you back or limiting you.

### Mute This Voice

**4**

- ✓ Turn the volume down on this voice.
- ✓ Focus instead on all the encouraging and positive voices, especially your voice of purpose.

### Amplify Your Voice of Purpose And Other Positive Voices

**5**

- ✓ Constantly surround yourself with other positive, encouraging voices.
- ✓ Build experiences that refute the negative voice, and use them to continuously amplify your voice of purpose and other positive voices.

# THE WORKBOOK

Awareness plays a pivotal role in being able to control your decisions. That is why in the workbook below, there are exercises focused on helping you to:

1.  Identify the dominant voices in the different areas of your life.

2.  Examine your positive and negative experiences, and how they may have set you on your current path.

3.  Identify your values, beliefs, hungers, and worldviews.

4.  Adapt your filters so that you can continue your journey in a fulfilling way.

5.  Identify and examine your voice of purpose, so that you can work on amplifying it.

At your own pace, go through the different sections in the workbook and carefully reflect on the questions below. It will help if you draw on the information from the first part, and on your answers to the reflections in the text. Take as much time as you need. If you find that you cannot answer any of the questions below, don't worry. This is a difficult step, but it is worth the effort. Consider revisiting this workbook as you work towards living a fulfilling and meaningful life.

***Good luck!***

# YOUR
# DOMINANT VOICES

**LIST THE DOMINANT VOICES IN THESE FOUR ASPECTS OF YOUR LIFE**

At home

At work

Your relationships

Dealing with yourself

# PERSONAL MAP OF THE MAIN VOICES

## FROM THE EARLIER EXERCISE, DETERMINE WHO THE MAIN VOICES AFFECTING YOUR DESCISIONS ARE

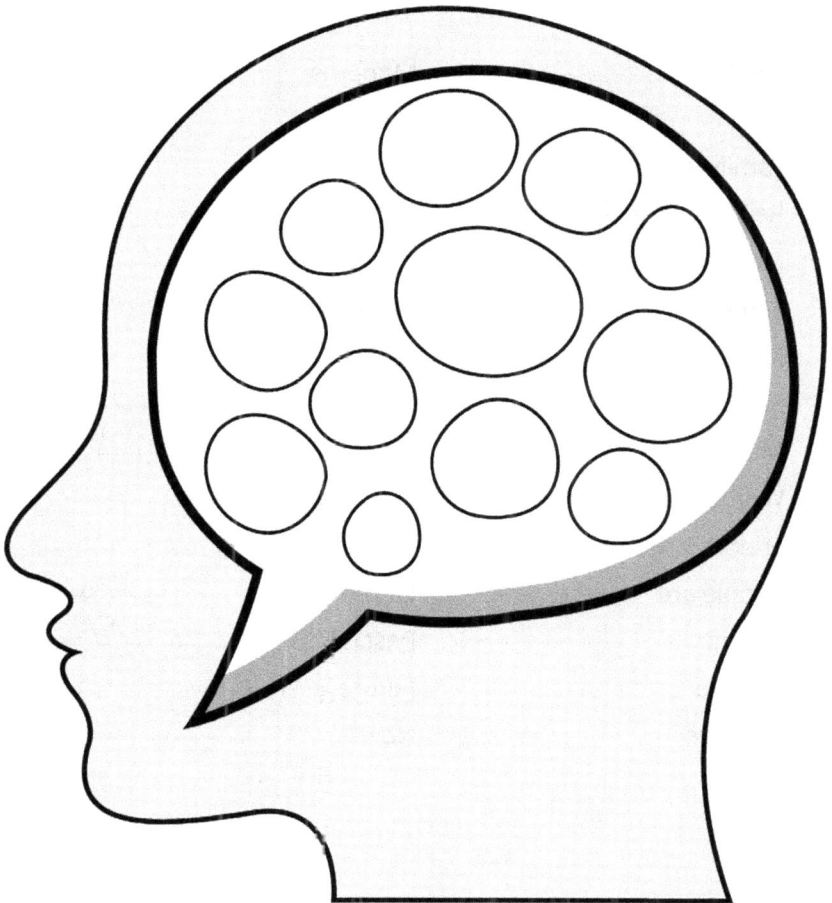

# YOUR WORLDVIEWS

**1. Write down the first word that comes to mind in describing your feeling about each word in this list:**

| | | | |
|---|---|---|---|
| Life is | .................... | Money is | .................... |
| Love is | .................... | Boss is | .................... |
| Family is | .................... | Colleagues are | .................... |
| Relatives are | .................... | Spouse is | .................... |
| Mother is | .................... | Children are | .................... |
| Father is | .................... | Problems are | .................... |
| Marriage is | .................... | Success is | .................... |
| Sex is | .................... | Failure is | .................... |
| Men are | .................... | Ambition is | .................... |
| Women are | .................... | Death is | .................... |
| Friends are | .................... | God is | .................... |
| People are | .................... | I am | .................... |
| Country is | .................... | Past is | .................... |
| Work is | .................... | Future is | .................... |
| Home is | .................... | Now is | .................... |

**2. Read your above answers as if they were someone else's answers, how would you describe that person?**

◯ Pessimist          ◯ Optimist

◯ Struggling Through Life          ◯ Cruizing Through Life

◯ Mostly Negative          ◯ Mostly Positive

**3. On a scale of 1 to 10, how happy do you believe this person is?**

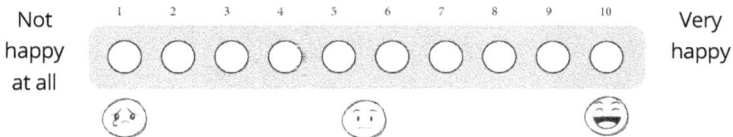

Not
happy
at all

| 1 | 2 | 3 | 4 | 5 | 6 | 7 | 8 | 9 | 10 |

◯ ◯ ◯ ◯ ◯ ◯ ◯ ◯ ◯ ◯

Very
happy

**4. What are the most striking issues this person has (which areas of this person's life cause the most intense emotions or views)?**

## 5. Which aspects of this person's views are the biggest sources of stress?

## 6. Which aspects of this person's views demand a change of perspective and interpretation?

**Limiting view**　　　　　　　　**alternative interpretation**

**7. Would you hire this person?**

Yes ⭘ No ⭘ Why: ........................................................

**8. Would you want to become friends with such a person?**

Yes ⭘ No ⭘ Why: ........................................................

**9. Would you want to spend your life with such a person?**

Yes ⭘ No ⭘ Why: ........................................................

**10. Which of these views offer hope, encouragement, growth and fulfillment?**

1. ........................................... 2. ...........................................

3. ........................................... 4. ...........................................

**11. Which of these views take away hope and discourage growth and fulfillment?**

1. ........................................... 2. ...........................................

3. ........................................... 4. ...........................................

**12. What would you advise such a person to do?**

**13. How can this person help him/herself?**

**14. How can this person get the necessary help to revisit the extreme interpretations?**

# YOUR VALUES

Our values can be defined as the objects, people, and principles that we hold in high regard, and that we place great emphasis on. We dedicate our time and our resources to them.  They filter the voices, so they affect how we make decisions. By extension, our values affect our lives.

1. Below is a comprehensive, but not exclusive, list of values. Go through them and see which ones you believe are part of your value system — put a (√) or (X) next to the ones that apply to you.

| | |
|---|---|
| 1. Achievement | 11. Contribution |
| 2. Adventure | 12. Control |
| 3. Ambition | 13. Courage |
| 4. Beauty | 14. Creativity |
| 5. Being the Best | 15. Curiosity |
| 6. Calmness | 16. Determination |
| 7. Cleanliness | 17. Discipline |
| 8. Comfort | 18. Empathy |
| 9. Compassion | 19. Excellence |
| 10. Competition | 20. Fairness |

21. Faith
22. Fame
23. Family
24. Friendship
25. Fulfillment
26. Fun
27. Happiness
28. Harmony
29. Health
30. Honesty
31. Humility
32. Independence
33. Integrity
34. Intelligence
35. Intimacy
36. Kindness
37. Knowledge
38. Love
39. Money
40. Nature

41. Neatness
42. Open-mindedness
43. Passion
44. Perfection
45. Persistence
46. Politeness
47. Power
48. Respect
49. Responsibility
50. Security
51. Spirituality
52. Spontaneity
53. Status
54. Strength
55. Success
56. Teamwork
57. Tolerance
58. Tradition
59. Truth
60. Wisdom

**2. Do you have any values that are not on the list? What are they?**

1. ........................................................
2. ........................................................

3. ........................................................
4. ........................................................

5. ........................................................
6. ........................................................

3. Now pick your top 10 values and rank them, with the highest value first:

1. ............................................................     2. ............................................................

3. ............................................................     4. ............................................................

5. ............................................................     6. ............................................................

7. ............................................................     8. ............................................................

9. ............................................................     10. ............................................................

4. Looking at your top 10 values, which ones would you categorize as:

| **Aspired values:** values you aspire to have now or in the future, and ones you feel would benefit you in the future | **Current values:** values that are part of your current value system and that affect your everyday decisions |
| --- | --- |
| | |

**5. Are there any values — current or aspired — that will not serve a beneficial purpose moving forward?**

Yes ⬭          No ⬭

If yes, what are these values? : ...........................................................

...................................................................................................................

...................................................................................................................

...................................................................................................................

...................................................................................................................

...................................................................................................................

**6. Which value(s) could you remove?**

**7. Now that you may have removed a few of your top 10 values, which value(s) would you add to your value system to elevate your life? Which value(s) do you believe would benefit your voice of purpose and your life?**

**8. Relist and rank your top 10 values in order of most valued to least:**

1. ......................................................

2. ......................................................

3. ......................................................

4. ......................................................

5. ......................................................

6. ......................................................

7. ......................................................

8. ......................................................

9. ......................................................

10. ......................................................

# YOUR EXPERIENCES

| What are the defining experiences that you had between the ages of: | What lessons, interpretations, beliefs, and worldviews did you form because of each of these experiences? |
|---|---|
| 3-10 years old: | |
| 11-20 years old: | |
| 21-30 years old: | |

| What are the defining experiences that you had between the ages of: | What lessons, interpretations, beliefs, and worldviews did you form because of each of these experiences? |
|---|---|
| 31-40 years old: | |
| 41-50 years old: | |
| 51-60 years old: | |
| 61 years old and onward: | |

2. Looking at the second column of the table above (your interpretations), which ones played a large role in shaping your life today?

A

B

C

D

3. Which of these interpretations of experiences encourage growth and fulfillment?

(A)          (B)          (C)          (D)

**4. Which ones need re-interpretation because time is proving they are not necessarily always true?**

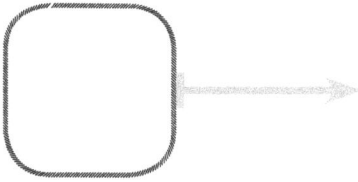

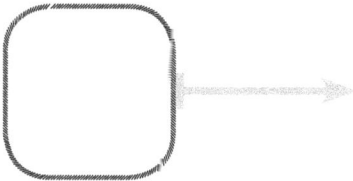

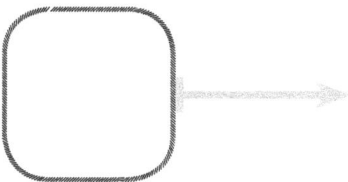

# YOUR BELIEFS

## 1. How lucky do you believe you are?

NOT AT ALL ◯    A LITTLE BIT ◯    AVERAGE ◯    QUITE A LOT ◯    VERY MUCH SO ◯

## 2. How good do you believe you are as a person?

NOT AT ALL ◯    A LITTLE BIT ◯    AVERAGE ◯    QUITE A LOT ◯    VERY MUCH SO ◯

## 3. How valuable do you believe your life is to you?

NOT AT ALL ◯    A LITTLE BIT ◯    AVERAGE ◯    QUITE A LOT ◯    VERY MUCH SO ◯

## 4. How valuable do you believe your life is to others?

NOT AT ALL ◯    A LITTLE BIT ◯    AVERAGE ◯    QUITE A LOT ◯    VERY MUCH SO ◯

## 5. How competent do you believe you are?

NOT AT ALL ◯    A LITTLE BIT ◯    AVERAGE ◯    QUITE A LOT ◯    VERY MUCH SO ◯

## 6. How pleasant and supportive do you believe you are in your relationships?

NOT AT ALL ◯    A LITTLE BIT ◯    AVERAGE ◯    QUITE A LOT ◯    VERY MUCH SO ◯

## 7. How valuable do you believe your work is?

NOT AT ALL ☐   A LITTLE BIT ☐   AVERAGE ☐   QUITE A LOT ☐   VERY MUCH SO ☐

## 8. What do you believe your future will be like?

VERY BAD ☐   BAD ☐   AVERAGE ☐   GOOD ☐   VERY GOOD ☐

## 9. In your last days, do you believe you will be:

ALONE ☐      SURROUNDED BY LOVED ONES ☐

## 10. In your last days, what do you believe your biggest regrets will be?

## 11. How do you believe you will be remembered?

**12. How much control do you believe you have over your life?**

NOT AT ALL ⃝   A LITTLE BIT ⃝   AVERAGE ⃝   QUITE A LOT ⃝   VERY MUCH SO ⃝

**13. Which of the above beliefs are negative?**

**14. Which of the negative beliefs do you see as fixed?**

**15. Why are you accepting this belief as a definite certainty?**

**16.  What would you say to your most loved ones if they had the same negative beliefs about themselves?**

**17. What would you advise them to do?**

**18. How can you apply the same advice to yourself and be an inspiration to your loved ones and to others?**

# YOUR HUNGERS

According to multiple psychologists, we all share similar basic needs that are part of our nature and are necessary for a healthy life.

When unmet, some of these needs might turn into hungers that trigger unhealthy behaviors.

**1. Select the top 10 needs that you feel are important to you**

## I NEED TO FEEL / BE:

Accepted

Accomplished

Acknowledged

Admired

Appreciated

Approved of

Believed in

Capable

Celebrated

Challenged

Clear (not confused)

Competent

Confident

Forgiven

Forgiving

Free

Fulfilled

Growing

Heard

Helped

Helpful

Important

In control
Included
Listened to
Loved
Needed
Noticed
Powerful
Private
Productive/Useful
Reassured
Recognized

Respected
Safe/Secure
Sexual
Supported
Touched
Treated Fairly
Trusted
Understanding
Understood
Valued
Worthy

**2. From the earlier exercise determine your top 3 dominant needs and fill in the below table:**

| YOUR TOP 3 NEEDS | How are these needs influencing mydecisions? | How are they influencing your relationships? | How are they influencing your work? |
|---|---|---|---|
| | | | |
| | | | |
| | | | |

| How are they influencing your level of happiness? | How are your currently feeding your needs ? | What are these mechanisms costing you? | How can you find healthy ways to deal with your hungers? |
|---|---|---|---|
|  |  |  |  |
|  |  |  |  |
|  |  |  |  |

**3. How can you feed them once and for all and become free?**

**4. How can you shield yourself from their negative impact?**

# YOUR VOICE OF PURPOSE

**1. Can you clearly notice your voice among all the other voices?**

Yes ☐               No ☐

**2. How would you describe your voice?**

**3. Does your voice clearly tell you what your authentic self thinks, feels, and hopes?**

Yes ☐               No ☐

**4. What does your authentic voice say about your professional life?**

5. What does your authentic voice say about your relationships with others?

6. What does your authentic voice say about your relationship with yourself?

7. Does your voice make itself heard to other voices?

Yes ⬭     No ⬭

8. How does your voice interact with the dominant voices?

**9. Is your voice assertive enough for others to hear what you say?**

Yes ⬭　　　　　　　No ⬭

**10. Which voices challenge your authentic voice the most?**

<br><br><br><br><br>

**11. To what extent does your voice lead your life?**

NOT AT ALL ⬭　　A LITTLE BIT ⬭　　AVERAGE ⬭　　QUITE A LOT ⬭　　VERY MUCH SO ⬭

**12. Are you fair in giving enough listening time to your voice as you do to other voices?**

NOT AT ALL ⬭　　A LITTLE BIT ⬭　　AVERAGE ⬭　　QUITE A LOT ⬭　　VERY MUCH SO ⬭

**13. Do you give more airtime to other voices than to your voice?**

Yes ⬭　　　　　　　No ⬭

Which Ones : ............................................................

........................................................................

........................................................................

........................................................................

........................................................................

**14. What can you do to make your authentic voice the most dominant voice?**

**15. How can you support your voice as it negotiates with other voices?**

# NOTES

**Introduction:**

Collin, Catherine, et al. *The psychology book: big ideas simply explained.* DK Publishers, 2012.

Frankl, Viktor E., et al. *Mans Search for Meaning.* Beacon Press, 2017.

"Maslow's Amazing Hierarchy." *UNICAF - Scholarship Programme,* 26 Oct. 2016, www.unicaf.org/maslows-amazing-hierarchy-of-needs/.

Soon, Chun Siong, et al. "Unconscious Determinants of Free Decisions in the Human Brain." Nature Neuroscience, vol. 11, no. 5, 2008, pp. 543–545., doi:10.1038/nn.2112.

**Chapter 1:**

Baggini, Julian. "Do Your Genes Determine Your Entire Life? | Julian Baggini." *The Guardian,* Guardian News and Media, 19 Mar. 2015, www.theguardian.com/science/2015/mar/19/do-your-genes-determine-your-entire-life.

Macdonald, Fiona. "Culture - Feral: The Children Raised by Wolves." *BBC News*, BBC, 12 Oct. 2015, www.bbc.com/culture/story/20151012-feral-the-children-raised-by-wolves.

Wong, Maggie Hiufu. "World's Longest Glass Bridge Opens in Hebei, China." *CNN*, Cable News Network, 5 Jan. 2018, edition.cnn.com/travel/article/hongyagu-glass-bridge-hebei-china/index.html.

## Chapter 2:

Aarts, Henk, et al. "Goal Contagion: Perceiving Is for Pursuing." *Journal of Personality and Social Psychology*, vol. 87, no. 1, 2004, pp. 23–37., doi:10.1037/0022-3514.87.1.23.

## Chapter 3:

Baggini, Julian. "Do Your Genes Determine Your Entire Life? | Julian Baggini." *The Guardian,* Guardian News and Media, 19 Mar. 2015, www.theguardian.com/science/2015/mar/19/do-your-genes-determine-your-entire-life.

Elias, Ric. "3 Things I Learned While My Plane Crashed." *TED: Ideas Worth Spreading,* www.ted.com/talks/ric_elias.

"Meryl Streep." Biography.com, *A&E Networks Television*, 3 Aug. 2018, www.biography.com/people/meryl-streep-9497266.

staff, Guardian. "CV of Failures: Princeton Professor Publishes Résumé of His Career Lows." *The Guardian,* Guardian News and Media, 30 Apr. 2016, www.theguardian.com/education/2016/apr/30/cv-of-failures-princeton-professor-publishes-resume-of-his-career-lows.

## Chapter 4:

Collin, Catherine, et al. *The psychology book: big ideas simply explained.* DK Publishers, 2012.

Harlow, Harry F. "Love in Infant Monkeys." *Scientific American,* vol. 200, no. 6, 1959, pp. 68-74, doi:10.1038/scientificamerican0659-68.

## Chapter 5:

"Grandma Moses." Biography.com, *A&E Networks Television,* 15 June 2016, www.biography.com/people/grandma-moses-9416251

Mead, Rebecca. "First at Ninety." *The New Yorker,* The New Yorker, 19 June 2017, www.newyorker.com/magazine/2007/09/17/first-at-ninety.

Moll, J., et al. "Human Fronto-Mesolimbic Networks Guide Decisions about Charitable Donation." *Proceedings of the National Academy of Sciences,* vol. 103, no. 42, Sept. 2006, pp. 15623–15628., doi:10.1073/pnas.0604475103.

Mutter, Reginald P.C. "Daniel Defoe." *Encyclopædia Britannica,* Encyclopædia Britannica, Inc., 17 Apr. 2018, www.britannica.com/biography/Daniel-Defoe.

O'Connor, Anahad. "The Claim: Identical Twins Have Identical Fingerprints." *The New York Times*, The New York Times, 2 Nov. 2004, www.nytimes.com/2004/11/02/health/the-claim-identical-twins-have-identical-fingerprints.html.

"Oprah Winfrey." Biography.com, *A&E Networks Television,* 21 May 2018, www.biography.com/people/oprah-winfrey-9534419

"Overview for Adeline De Walt Reynolds." *Turner Classic Movies,* www.tcm.com/tcmdb/person/160572%7C7494/Adeline-deWalt-Reynolds/.

Schnall, Simone, et al. "Elevation Leads to Altruistic Behavior." *Psychological Science,* vol. 21, no. 3, 2010, pp. 315–320., doi:10.1177/0956797609359882.

TEDxTalks. "What's Your Prison?: Paul Wood at TEDxAuckland." *YouTube,* YouTube, 5 Dec. 2012, www.youtube.com/watch?v=LjjlsW1MDmc.

"The Man Who Single-Handedly Carved A Road Through a Mountain to Help His Village." *Good News Network,* 30 July 2017, www.goodnewsnetwork.org/man-single-handedly-carved-road-mountain/.

"Timeline." *Julia Child Foundation,* juliachildfoundation.org/timeline/.

"Wolfgang Mozart." Biography.com, *A&E Networks Television,* 28 Apr. 2017, www.biography.com/people/wolfgang-mozart-9417115.

**Workbook:**

Pavlina, Steve. "List of Values." *Steve Pavlina,* 10 Apr. 2016, www.stevepavlina.com/blog/2004/11/list-of-values/.

## *About The Author*

Michael Kouly began his career as a Reuters war journalist.
He covered armed conflicts that
involved, Israel, Lebanon, Syria,
Iran, Hezbullah, Islamic extrem-
ists, terrorism, the United States,
Kuwait, Iraq and others... He also
covered musical concerts, fash-
ion shows and car racing.

Writing about wars, geopol-
itics, international diplomacy, and global events offered
Michael unique opportunities to witness, analyze and
write about leadership at the highest levels: where bad
leadership meant the loss of thousands of lives and good
leadership led to avoiding wars, saving lives and rebuild-
ing shattered countries.

Michael also exercised corporate leadership over a period of 30 years as he led the growth of regional and international businesses. He is a three-time CEO and president
at organizations like Reuters, Orbit and Cambridge Insti-

tute for Global Leadership, managing people in more than 20 countries.

Over the span of his career, Michael made some good decisions that generated remarkable success and also some not so good decisions that offered valuable lessons on what works and what doesn't when exercising leadership - emphasizing the mindset of "you either win or learn".

From  as far back as he can remember, Michael has been fascinated by leadership. He has spent his life learning about leadership, purpose and strategy by practicing them, watching others lead and by conducting extensive research on the art and science of mobilizing people and organizations towards growth and noble purposes.

Michael is a World Bank Fellow, author and keynote speaker about leadership, strategy, purpose and international politics. He is the founder of the Kouly Institute and the creator of unique Executive Leadership Programs, that have been delivered to thousands of top business executives, NGO's and government leaders worldwide.

He also dedicates time to various non-profit organizations such as the Middle East Leadership Academy (MELA), Central Eurasia Leadership Academy (CELA), South East Asia Leadership Academy (SEALA) and Leaders Across Boarders (LAB).

His calling is to help people, organizations and countries lead purpose driven lives.

Michael studied at Harvard and Princeton Universities, and is an advisor to state leaders.

# OTHER BOOKS BY THE AUTHOR

## BOOK 1 OF THE
## SELF-LEADERSHIP BOOK SERIES

# FINDING YOUR HUMMUS

**This book will provide you, your colleagues, family and friends with insights about life and business to unleash your personal and organizational power.**

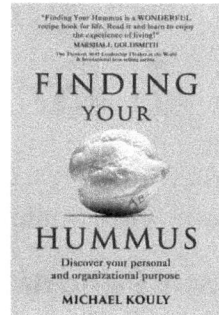

• Shift happens in life and business, are you ready?

• What is the prime philosophy behind starting a business of growth and sustainable success?

• Do you, your people and business have a guiding purpose? This book is about finding your calling.

• Do you have a personal and organizational strategy to fulfill your purpose? This book is about self-awareness, self-motivation and self-leadership that together can achieve self-fulfillment.

• How do you deal with competition, conflict and confusion? This book is rich with empowering inspirational quotes that generate strength and lead to self-actualization.

• What is the mindset to lead a life of resilience, abundance and significance? This book is about finding your passion and discovering your way of living a purpose driven life.

## BOOK 2 OF THE
## SELF-LEADERSHIP BOOK SERIES

# If I didn't
# Give A ....
# I would...

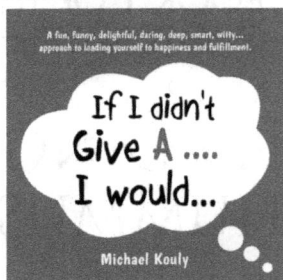

> A fun, funny, delightful, daring, deep, smart, witty...
> approach to leading yourself to happiness and fulfillment.
>
> **If I didn't**
> **Give A ....**
> **I would...**
>
> Michael Kouly

**As you will discover, this entertaining book of insightful and witty humor is not like other self leadership books.**

### WHILE ENJOYING THE EXPERIENCE OF THIS BOOK, YOU'LL ALSO:

- **Blow off steam:** We all have personal issues, challenges, and obstacles that accumulate stress that must be released to keep us in a state of peak motivation.

- **Know yourself:** Sometimes an entire life is spent being stuck at the expense of personal, business, social and relational opportunities for success. Self-discovery is the first step to the healing, actualization, and optimization of your life.

- **Reflect:** Recognizing your priorities, what you really want and what matters most to you is the key to your growth in all aspects of your life.

- **Decide:** To solve problems and catch opportunities, decisions are needed. This book will help you decide and act to expand your potential in a fun, playful, smart and effective way.

- **Lead:** True leadership starts with the self where smart and effective strategy, action and execution are the keys to the growth of our capacity.

# WIDE OPEN

**Leadership is a dangerous enterprise, but the rewards are valuable. This book is designed to be your companion in your thrilling journey of remarkable survival and outstanding growth.**

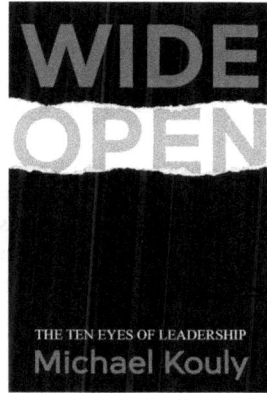

THE TEN EYES OF LEADERSHIP
Michael Kouly

## THIS UNIQUE AND ILLUMINATING BOOK WILL OPEN YOUR EYES WIDE, SO YOU LEARN MORE ABOUT:

- **Authority:** You are surrounded by authority figures such as parents, bosses, CEOs, presidents, or governments. As you already know, not understanding how to deal with authority is risky.

- **Enemies:** Enemies are a fact of life. They could be passive or aggressive. Enemies want to undermine you and your acts of leadership. Not understanding how to deal with enemies is dangerous.

- **Understanding Yourself and Others:** It is hard to survive and grow and to lead yourself without understanding what drives your thoughts, feelings, words, actions, behaviors, dreams, and ambitions. It is impossible to lead others without understanding them first.

- **Understanding Systems:** We live and work in systems. A system can be a family, team, company, community, city, country or the world. Systems have their unique psychology and rules. Not understanding systems will put your existence and progress at risk, as you may be excluded or isolated from the group that you belong to.

HOW TO
# TRUMP THE ENEMY

**Some people love you and some don't. When you exercise leadership, some will support you and others will resist, oppose, obstruct, sabotage, or obsessively fight you until you lose.**

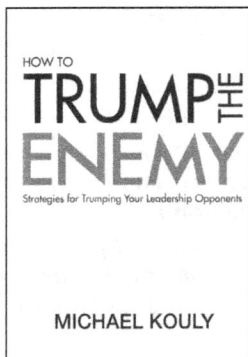

HOW TO
TRUMP THE ENEMY
Strategies for Trumping Your Leadership Opponents

MICHAEL KOULY

**Most attempts at leadership fail not because of how allies are utilized, but because many leaders lack the vital skills necessary for dealing with adversaries.**

**What will determine your leadership success is mainly your ability to handle those who stand against you.**

**THIS BOOK IS A UNIQUE AND COMPREHENSIVE REFERENCE THAT YOU CAN CONSULT EVERY TIME YOU DEAL WITH RESISTERS, OPPONENTS, OR ENEMIES.**

**YOU WILL LEARN MORE ABOUT:**

- **Strategies:** There are 104 strategies that you can use separately or in combinations as per the specific nature of the resistance that you are facing.

- **Scenarios:** There are 36 separate scenarios covering seven types of personal, social, organizational, business, and political opponents.

- **Intensities:** There are six intensities of opposition that start from passive and escalate to passive-aggressive, active, active-aggressive, malevolent, and finally archenemy.

- **You:** There is a chapter on YOU acting as your own enemy by allowing your dysfunctional mindsets, beliefs, and habits to sabotage your growth and prevent you from being all that you can be.

*In The Making...*
# New Titles
*by Michael Kouly*

# FORGET
## HAPPINESS

**MICHAEL KOULY**
**FORGET**
HAPPINESS

Seven Steps to a Fulfilled Life

**Read this book and fill your life with joy.**

*You deserve it.*

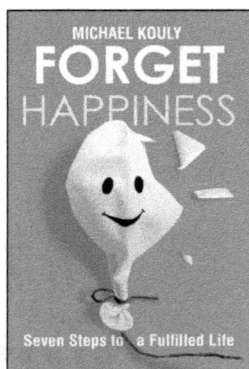

This unique book offers a practical, clear, and realistic roadmap for reaching fulfillment. It is a pleasant and easy read that will lift your spirits, encourage you, and help you discover and love your beautiful self so that you may live a life of purpose, meaning, beauty, and joy.

We live in the most comfortable and exciting time in history, and yet stress, anxiety, depression, suffering, and inner emptiness are greater than ever before, even among the rich and successful. Happiness has become a tired buzzword. An increasing number of self-help books idealize and promise it, yet it remains frustratingly elusive.

This book asks you to stop looking for happiness because happiness cannot be found on its own. Happiness is an outcome, a result, a consequence of living a life of fulfillment. When you align your life with your true self and feel fulfilled, deep happiness, joy, and inner peace will become part of your natural state.

# BEYOND
# STRATEGY

## WHY "BEYOND STRATEGY"?

**Many people find strategy intimidating, complex, or abstract, but it doesn't have to be.**

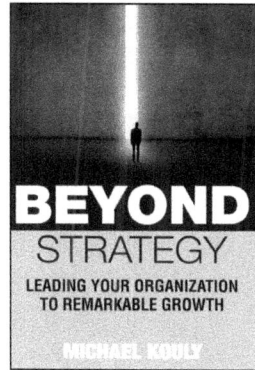

BEYOND
STRATEGY
LEADING YOUR ORGANIZATION
TO REMARKABLE GROWTH
MICHAEL KOULY

This book presents a new way of thinking about strategy that is uniquely based upon the Purpose-Driven Growth Model (PDG), in which your organization's purpose and profitability is key to guiding its growth.

- It explores strategy concisely and thoughtfully, examining what the concept encompasses and how strategies can be constructed in a fast-changing and uncertain world.

- It illustrates the differences between strategies that flourish and strategies that languish, and delves into the reasons driving each outcome.

- It offers comprehensive thinking, and tools which view strategy holistically, emphasizing how to lead organizations towards sustainable growth and exceptional performance.

The PDG Model sketches out a practical hybrid of strategy and leadership, that must be unified to fulfill organzational purpose, create growth, and deliver profits. Leadership without strategy is futile, and strategy without leadership is doomed. The two must synchronize to produce results.